James Joyce

W. Y. TINDALL

James Joyce

HIS WAY OF INTERPRETING

THE MODERN WORLD

CHARLES SCRIBNER'S SONS, NEW YORK

CHARLES SCRIBNER'S SONS, LTD., LONDON

1950

14414

TO ELIZABETH

ACKNOWLEDGMENTS

I am very grateful to Mr. B. W. Huebsch and The Viking Press for permission to quote from *Finnegans Wake, A Portrait of the Artist as a Young Man,* and *Chamber Music;* to New Directions for permission to quote from *Stephen Hero;* and to Rinehart & Company, Inc., for permission to quote from Herbert Gorman's *James Joyce.* Passages from James Joyce's *Ulysses,* copyright, 1914, 1918, 1942, 1946 by Norah Joseph Joyce, are reprinted by permission of Random House, Inc.

For aid with *Finnegans Wake* I am greatly indebted to James Gilvarry, one of the principal authorities. Many of my facts and interpretations are his. Nathan Halper, to whom I owe as much, helped me to reach an opinion about the structure of the book and gave me insight into several puzzling matters. All those who, sitting at long oblong tables with me, talked of myth and symbol or read *Finnegans Wake* deserve my gratitude. William Bridgwater and Hiram Haydn, who read my manuscript, improved it by their learning and reduced the number of errors. I thank them; and I owe more than I can say to Elizabeth and Cecilia for faith, hope, and charity.

W. Y. T.

New York
June 16, 1949

CONTENTS

INTRODUCTION

IN 1924 Edmund Gosse, the dean of English critics, exposed the worthlessness, impudence, and indecency of Joyce, a man not entirely without talent perhaps, but "a literary charlatan of the extremest order." *Ulysses,* Gosse continued, is "an anarchical production, infamous in taste, in style, in everything . . . There are no English critics of weight or judgment who consider Mr. Joyce an author of any importance." These remarks are typical of conservative opinion at that time. Even younger critics sometimes ignored Joyce or, when they noticed him, condescended a little.

It is easier for us than it was for these traditionalists to see Joyce as part of the great tradition extending from Dante to Ibsen and Rimbaud. It is easier for us to see how, within that tradition, Joyce made something important and new. Today he is generally recognized as one of the great writers of our time.

It still seems necessary, however, to defend him against the charge of obscurity. He is difficult, to be sure, but only as those who have many things to say are difficult. There is no sign in his work of willful obscurity. Like Beethoven and Picasso he advanced from the simple to the complex as he adapted his method to expanding needs.

His early works have a simple narrative level. In *Ulysses* the narrative level is complicated by symbols and techniques that sometimes interfere with easy reading. These complications are not so much of an obstacle as some suppose. Indeed, there is little in the book that a careful reading will not discover. Even what a careless reading gives us is of value, and, with rereading,

1

other things of greater value appear. I judge these matters by my own experience.

When I finished college in 1925, my mother and father sent me out to see the world. I knew enough about it to go to Paris. Although my teachers at college had shielded me from contemporary literature, I had heard talk of *Ulysses* among the more dubious undergraduates, none of whom had seen a copy. As soon as I reached Paris, I hurried to the rue de l'Odéon, and, conscious of a great experience before me, bought the blue-covered volume. In the gardens of the Luxembourg, where I read that book, my misunderstanding of it did little to interfere with my pleasure. *Ulysses* seemed rich, strange, and thoroughly satisfying. Since that tremendous day in June—it happened to be the 16th of the month, the day that is celebrated in *Ulysses*—I have read the book again and again, each time with more understanding and delight. If I could enjoy it without the aid of commentaries and with no equipment to speak of except some acquaintance with Sir Thomas Browne and Edward Gibbon, I conclude that *Ulysses* is suitable for the common reader.

It may seem that *Finnegans Wake* has less to occupy the attention while the book does its work. But like a good poem, it has sound and rhythm and meanings not far beneath the surface. After the reader has enjoyed these sounds and rhythms and mastered these meanings, he can descend to other meanings without too much trouble. The seasoned reader closes the book with the feeling that there is nothing better—or, indeed, more necessary—to do than to read it over again.

The value of a book depends less upon the amount of reality it contains than upon the amount of reality under control. Insight into reality has little value unless the author discovers a form that is adequate. Joyce seems to have understood everything—even women—and he excelled in forms expressing what he understood. His formal vision, uniting our intellectual and aesthetic interests, presents all our reality.

Joyce's effect upon our ways of thinking, feeling, and expressing ourselves proves his success in what he undertook. His effect upon our minds has been almost as pervasive as that of

Einstein or of Freud. Whereas their effect has been upon thinking, Joyce's has been upon thinking and feeling at once; for he was not a philosopher but an artist. An artist's way of knowing, although different from a philosopher's, is of equal importance. Few literate people today, whether novelists, poets, dramatists, critics, or readers, have altogether escaped the influence of his forms. His ways of knowing, like those of Einstein and Freud, have become ours.

Joyce gave novelists their methods for exploring the interior of man. Although he did not invent the stream of consciousness, he made it a usable technique. Although he did not invent the symbol, he showed novelists how to use it for expressing what they cannot state. It is he who is directly responsible for the many-leveled novel and story that have almost displaced the simple narrative. Because of his achievement the commonest reader today is accustomed to indirections and to odd concords of inner and outer, of past and present, of particular and general.

Perhaps his most important effect has been upon the word. Under his spell, novelists, writing more and more like poets, use the word to evoke. Depending upon suggestion rather than statement, they express the overtones of experience while they fix its meaning and quality by rhythms.

The word-formations and rhythms of Joyce have also had their effect upon recent poets, upon Dylan Thomas, for example, and Lawrence Durrell, two of the best poets of England. Thomas Merton, whose poems are Joycean, says that Joyce helped convert him to Catholicism. This effect, however, is less obvious than the rest.

Joyce's most famous follower was Virginia Woolf, whose *Mrs. Dalloway* and *To the Lighthouse,* two of the finest novels of our time, owe not only their techniques but their themes to Joyce. In America, Thomas Wolfe drew theme and method for *Look Homeward, Angel* from the tattered first edition of *Ulysses* that he kept eccentrically upon his icebox. But almost all our important novelists—Steinbeck, Faulkner, Malcolm Lowry, and Dos Passos—have drawn freely upon Joyce. In *Raintree County* Ross Lockridge adapted *Ulysses* to the requirements of the best seller. We cannot join a book club or visit a lending library without encountering Joyce.

It would be easy enough to give other examples and to describe the effect of Joyce upon dramatists and critics. But the effect upon readers is more important. Joyce has created a demand for literature which is not an escape from life but its central expression. Because of what he did, readers demand a multi-dimensional literature that presents the complexity of our time. They demand many-sided characters and words with many meanings.

It is true that part of the poetic complexity of our desire is due to others than Joyce—to Freud and Dostoevsky, James and Proust. But because Joyce gave the most adequate expression to what concerns us, he is chiefly responsible for our desire. When he described the poet as "the intense centre of the life of his age," he had himself in mind; for he had what Aristotle calls magnanimity and Aquinas calls pride. The poet alone, Joyce continued, "is capable of absorbing in himself the life that surrounds him and of flinging it abroad again amid planetary music."

CHAPTER ONE

DAEDALUS

THE works of Joyce compose an elaborate design. *A Portrait of the Artist as a Young Man* grows out of *Dubliners*. Far greater than these and more complex, *Ulysses* grows out of them. *Finnegans Wake* is a development of *Ulysses*. Even the minor works, such as *Chamber Music* and *Exiles,* take their place in the enormous pattern. Intricacies of shape and the connections of part with part make this pattern seem another labyrinth.

Joyce had the original labyrinth in mind. *A Portrait of the Artist* begins with a quotation from the eighth book of *Metamorphoses*. In these lines and those that precede them Ovid tells how Daedalus made the labyrinth and, after that, made wings. Naming his hero Stephen Dedalus, Joyce undertook to rival and maybe to surpass the "fabulous artificer." What Ovid calls the "unknown arts" of Daedalus symbolized for Joyce his own designs.

The tenth chapter of *Ulysses* is the book's epitome. In this chapter, which Joyce called "labyrinthine," he displays the city of Dublin. Wandering its streets, citizens and readers alike are confused by false leads, stopped by dead ends, and deceived by similarities. Stephen Dedalus and heroic Mr. Bloom, hunting clues, appear as unimportant as the man in the brown macintosh. Their city, which suggests more than the art of making labyrinths, is Joyce's vision of reality or, at least, of part of it.

Elsewhere the citizens seem more important than their city, and it becomes clear that the labyrinth is also man. Stephen and Mr. Bloom are more confusing than the streets they follow.

5

Whereas the streets maintain one level, these heroes, existing simultaneously on many levels, go off in several directions. Stephen and Mr. Bloom are limited by time—for *Ulysses* is the story of a single day—but H. C. Earwicker, the hero of *Finnegans Wake*, is limited by neither time nor space. His labyrinth makes that of Daedalus seem almost simple-minded.

By the art of flight, the second of his unknown arts, Joyce understood not only art but flight. *Dubliners,* his book of stories, explains his reasons for taking-off. Comprising what he called a chapter in the moral history of Ireland, these stories deal with decay. What they exhale, of course, is "the special odour of corruption." The worldly priest, the sentimental patriot, the pathetic laundress, and all the cruel, dishonest or frustrated people of *Dubliners* form an arrangement of the living-dead. It is not accidental that the little boy of the first story in the book is fascinated by the word "paralysis." Suggestions of Dante's hell and the presence of the seven sins help prove the kinship of Joyce's Dubliners with Baudelaire's Parisians and the Londoners of Eliot's *Waste Land.*

As Ovid's Daedalus, fleeing from Crete, said that although Minos might block escape by land and sea, "yet the sky is open, and by that way will I go," so Joyce, fleeing his nation, makes Stephen Dedalus echo his mythical predecessor: "When the soul of a man is born in this country there are nets flung at it to hold it back from flight. You talk to me of nationality, language, religion. I shall try to fly by those nets."

From his refuge on the Continent Joyce addressed two rhymed epistles to his countrymen. In *The Holy Office,* the first of these, announcing his flight, he denounced those who "crouched and crawled and prayed." In *Gas from a Burner,* the second, he praised his native land as a place where Christ and Caesar are hand in glove:

> This lovely land that always sent
> Her writers and artists to banishment
> And in a spirit of Irish fun
> Betrayed her own leaders, one by one.

These Swiftian verses raise a question: was Joyce a satirist? Passages in *Dubliners* and the greater works seem to be satiric, and in his letters Joyce sometimes spoke of sharpening his pen to write about those who had betrayed him. Destroying the chandelier in the brothel scene of *Ulysses*, Stephen hears "ruin of all space, shattered glass and toppling masonry." This symbolic cataclysm includes light or God, and by association with Stephen's mother and father, Church and country. A satirist's severity seems implicit. But in *A Portrait of the Artist* Stephen is shown sublimating personal anger into impersonal vision, "reshaping the world about him into a vision of squalor and insincerity. Yet his anger lent nothing to the vision. He chronicled with patience what he saw, detaching himself from it." While it is true that both Stephen and Joyce were sometimes petulant and driven by their troubles to hold the Irish up to scorn, it is as true that on the whole Joyce's work, however ironic about departures from the good and the true, is comparatively free from savage laughter or moral indignation. His vision is far less satiric than contemplative, less destructive or edifying than creative. Less concerned with what is wrong with man than with the nature of man and the power of creation, Joyce was true to Stephen's vow: "He would create proudly out of the freedom and power of his soul, as the great artificer whose name he bore, a living thing, new and soaring and beautiful, impalpable, imperishable."

For an Irishman with this desire one course alone seemed open. "Isolation," says Stephen, "is the first principle of artistic economy." Impossible in Ireland, isolation led to exile. Joyce's exile may have been the recognition of necessity, but he had good precedent for flight. Besides Daedalus, there were Blake, Byron, Shelley, Baudelaire, and Rimbaud, all favorites of his, and poets whose example had all the weight of the romantic tradition behind it. For over a hundred years artists, confronted with the hostility or indifference of the ruling class, had retired within themselves or fled. Even more attractive than this tradition were the examples of Dante, Swift, and Ibsen. These above all other writers were his models in art and life, and each of these was in some sort an exile. To his hot adolescence Ibsen seemed worthiest of devotion. Joyce learned Danish to read Ibsen, and in that language wrote him a letter of praise for "absolute indifference to public canons of art." Ibsen, the letter continues, has walked in lonely heroism a path which Joyce undertakes to follow—and maybe to go farther than the master himself.

This youthful extravagance, which seems less absurd to us than it might have seemed to a contemporary, is a promise of the almost terrible integrity with which, after setting his course, Joyce imprudently pursued it. To a man of such integrity, both moral and aesthetic, exile was the best means to an end.

In order to create he needed freedom. This meant not only freedom from the restrictions with which Ireland surrounds her writers, but that detachment from a subject which is necessary in order to master it. Ireland was one of Joyce's subjects. For contemplation as well as mastery, distance was needed. It was partly to gain Ireland that he left it. As Stephen remarks in his diary, "the shortest way to Tara was *via* Holyhead."

In *A Portrait of the Artist as a Young Man* Joyce presents the making of an exile. The art that makes this autobiographical novel the best of its kind may be admired by comparing it with *Stephen Hero,* part of an early version of *A Portrait of the Artist.* Where *Stephen Hero* is loosely composed, literal, and unselective, *A Portrait of the Artist* is at once suggestive and final. Between the two versions Joyce had changed. As the writer of the first he was a young man and as the writer of the second an artist. But where the versions overlap, the matter of both is generally the same. Both follow the moral, intellectual, and aesthetic development of an extraordinary boy.

When Joyce undertook his self-portrait, the novel of adolescence or of apprenticeship to life and art was not uncommon. For over a hundred years artists had chosen this form to define their quarrel with the world and to affirm their sensibility. Exiles, who by their separation from other men were forced to contemplate and justify themselves, found this form inevitable. Winning almost universal applause, Samuel Butler's *Way of All Flesh,* inspired many imitations. That Joyce's book, like Maugham's *Of*

Human Bondage, is one of these is likely. But Joyce was on even more familiar terms with *Wilhelm Meister* and *Richard Feverel.* Tradition offered a form in which he easily surpassed his predecessors.

A Portrait of the Artist is divided into two parts, the first concerning Stephen's development under the influence of family, nation, and religion, the second his escape from them. To Stephen, the "tyranny of home" means squalor and parents. In the family kitchen he finds pawn tickets, louse marks, and watery tea. His father, a witty, improvident man, becomes identified in Stephen's mind with the fatherland; his mother, who is devoted to his spiritual salvation, becomes identified with the Church. Ignoring the claims of sentiment and gratitude, Stephen tries to turn his back upon what has given him life and helped to shape it.

His father is a Parnellite, and Stephen's earliest memories are of political squabbles. The betrayal of Parnell disgusts Stephen with politics and the national revival. While at school he is surrounded by Gaelic enthusiasts and adorers of peasants. But Gaelic seems to threaten the final separation of Ireland from European culture, and peasants, who seem dull, pious, and commercial, leave him cold. He abandons the class in Gaelic after a single session. As for England, the object of national hatred, he remains indifferent to it.

These national and domestic surroundings have greater effect upon him than he knows, but he is certain of the power of religion. His mother's influence and a Jesuit education make him so obedient that he is chosen Prefect of the Sodality of the Blessed Virgin. But adolescence brings with it a deadly sin and in its train the other six. At this point the Jesuit fathers hold a retreat for the examination of conscience. Coldly and systematically, after the formula of Ignatius Loyola, the priest describes the odors, sights, and sounds of hell and all its pains. Stephen vomits. Horror and "the sting of conscience" drive him to the sacrament of penance. Refusing to scratch the bites of fleas, he is ascetic and austere. If Joyce had ended hereabouts, *A Portrait of the Artist* would be the great Catholic novel; for nothing on spiritual experience in recent literature is more moving, authentic, and exemplary. But Stephen tires of pieties, and when the Jesuits, noticing his Jesuitical demeanor, ask him to become one of their number, he declines. The trouble is that the Church fails to conform to his high ideal of what a church should be. Not he but the Church is insufficiently Catholic. For Stephen's difficult case, a Jesuit advises a clerkship in Guinness's brewery.

Stephen's schoolfellows, representing a conspiracy of Church and State, have shown him what an Irish heresy-hunt can be. "Admit," they cry, and this word joins "submit" among Stephen's horrors. Dramatizing himself as Lucifer, that more splendid rebel, and as Byron perhaps, Stephen exclaims, "I will not serve." Elsewhere he expands this refusal: "I will not serve that in which I no longer believe, whether it call itself my home, my fatherland or my church." As heretic and outlaw, condemned to loneliness, with only arrogance as his support, he leaves "the house of prayer and prudence into which he had been born and the order of life out of which he had come."

Before this, however, he has experienced what amounts to a religious conversion in reverse, a conversion to the world. On the beach one afternoon, as the boys shout his symbolic name and as a girl wades in the water, he becomes aware of mortal beauty. This apprehension is followed by an almost mystical ecstasy. His enlargement and sense of dedication more than compensate for the prospect of loneliness. Knowing it is not in his nature to correct or to improve society, he dedicates himself to creating the "uncreated experience" of his race.

Joyce remained obsessed with what he had rejected. Religion and family joined nation among his literary preoccupations. It is only natural that he became obsessed with exile.

Alienation is a principal theme of *Ulysses*. Having been grounded after his first flight, Stephen is gloomily preparing for another; but Mr. Bloom's condition is more desperate. Mr. Bloom is not only a symbol of the middle class but a symbolic exile from it. A Jew, never accepted by the society for which he yearns, he is sneered at, violently persecuted by the Citizen, continually frustrated or ignored, and, in spite of his friendliness, snubbed by

Mr. Menton. He suffers his wife's admirers because through them he enjoys a kind of relationship with other men.

The hero of "A Painful Case" in *Dubliners,* almost as lonely as "lovelorn longlost lugubru Booloohoom," is an exile from life. Fear and refinement have made him withdraw, like the hero of Henry James' "Beast in the Jungle," from proffered experience. His particular anguish is that sense of loss and the guilt which attend those who are separate.

Shem, the Stephen of *Finnegans Wake,* is also identified with the hero of "A Painful Case" and with Mr. Bloom. Not the least among wild geese, as Irish exiles are called, he has waged a "penisolate war" with society. Part of his story of loneliness and guilt is set to the tune of Thomas Campbell's "Exile of Erin," and his fate is implied in distortions of the phrase "securus iudicat orbis terrarum." This thematic refrain comes from St. Augustine's comment on exiles: "The calm judgment of the world is that those men cannot be good who in any part of the world cut themselves off from the rest of the world." Rarely calm, this judgment is also visited upon Shem's father, H. C. Earwicker, who, to the customers of his pub, appears as outlandish as Mr. Bloom. The plight of Earwicker and Bloom, exiles at home, is so exemplary that wild geese like Shem and Stephen seem fortunate.

Since such dwellers in the "downandoutermost" are preoccupied with home, it is not surprising that home in the sense of family became central in Joyce's work. Joyce was a family man—one who stays home at night or carries a hamper on Sundays. Thomas Wolfe was once astonished to meet his idol, followed by wife and children and carrying the hamper, on the field of Waterloo. Whether the family which is celebrated in *Finnegans Wake* and in *Ulysses* is primarily Joyce's own or his father's is of no importance; for the two became one in his mind. The family he had tried to escape was reencountered daily at breakfast or supper.

Joyce's concern was with the interrelationships among parents and children or between husband and wife. In "The Dead," the last story of *Dubliners,* Gabriel and his wife are happy enough at the party, but on the way home and at the hotel each becomes aware not so much of a change in their relationship as of its emptiness. Although Mr. and Mrs. Bloom of *Ulysses* live in the same house, they have been estranged since the death of their son. Mr. Bloom is recessive, and Mrs. Bloom, surrounded by lovers, is dominant. During the course of that day, however, his attitude toward her changes, partly because of his meeting with a substitute son and partly because of his attainment of equanimity. She will never change, but since he has changed a little, their relationship will be different. He who has always brought her breakfast to her bed orders her to bring him his. It matters little that she probably will not do it. He has enjoyed his triumph. During the night of *Finnegans Wake* a change takes place between Mr. and Mrs. Earwicker. He becomes centered in his children, in Kevin, his son, and Isabel, his daughter. The book ends with Mrs. Earwicker's pathetic cry, "you're changing from me, I can feel . . . for a daughter-wife from the hills again."

Exiles, a play by the "home cured emigrant," presents a more complicated family situation. The theme is Richard Rowan's simultaneous desire and reluctance to allow his wife the freedom in which he believes. His dilemma is complicated by two attachments, one to his mother and the other to his art. Whether or not his wife has spent the night with Robert is of little interest; for Richard alone occupies the stage among shadows. It matters more that his internal tensions, which constitute the drama, are unresolved and we are left unsatisfied. This apparently morbid document was modelled faithfully, but maybe not faithfully enough, upon Ibsen's *When We Dead Awaken,* on which Joyce had written an essay, praising the master for the perception of great truths and the opening of great questions or conflicts. Joyce's failure to dramatize the questions and conflicts he opened kept him from achieving what he was to call "Ibscenest nansence." (In this ambiguity from *Finnegans Wake* he alludes to Ibsen's exploratory power and to his reception by the public.)

An equal obsession with the Church is apparent in most of Joyce's works. "I am a product of Catholicism," says Stephen, and his friend Cranly observes: "It is a curious thing . . . how your mind is supersaturated with the religion in which you say you disbelieve." This saturation defines Stephen throughout *Ulysses*. As he walks the streets, he intones fragments of the Mass. When drunk in the maternity hospital, he learnedly mixes canon law with irreverence. Says Mulligan: "You have the cursed jesuit strain in you, only it's injected the wrong way." But blasphemy, as T. S. Eliot remarks, is closer to belief than indifference.

According to Shaun, *Finnegans Wake* consists of "nothing but clerical horrors." There is much in what he says. The tremendous volume seems composed of parodies of liturgy from the Credo to the Office of the Blessed Virgin. Time is told by the canonical hours. In this setting, exile is transformed into excommunication. Refusing to become a Jesuit and going instead into the "society of Jewses," Shem has sold his birthright for "messes of mottage." But when he says, "There's no plagues like Rome," the nostalgia is inescapable.

The hero of *Stephen Hero* tells himself: "In temper and mind you are still a Catholic. Catholicism is in your blood." In this sense Joyce is the most Catholic writer of our time. But for all the apparatus of religion, there is no religion here. Joyce is opposite to D. H. Lawrence, who had religion without its apparatus.

"Jesuistical" Joyce could neither live in nor forget his city. "Was liffe worth leaving?" he asks in *Finnegans Wake;* but only his body ever left the Liffey, and Joyce, like Shem, remained a "doblinganger" or a "ghost by absence" like the Shakespeare imagined by Stephen in *Ulysses*. But for nationalism this nostalgic spirit would have been a nationalist. His work is as crowded with Irish history from the Firbolgs to Sinn Fein as with the sights, sounds, and smells of Dublin or with the seven sacraments. In *Ulysses,* Mr. Bloom is puzzled by Stephen's remark that Ireland must be important because it belongs to him. "This race and this country and this life produced me," he says in *A Portrait of the Artist*. "I shall express myself as I am." In this sense Joyce is the most Irish writer of our time. It was he who raised Dublin, where *Ulysses* is still forbidden, from the seventh city of Christendom to the first city of contemporary literature.

John Eglinton, however, saw in Joyce's work a violent interruption to the Irish literary renaissance, and it becomes necessary to examine his connection with that movement. A Catholic among Anglo-Irish writers, Joyce read nothing of their work until he was at Belvedere College. Then he discovered Yeats and admired him to the point of committing his stories as well as his poems to memory. *A Portrait of the Artist* tells how at the opening night of *The Countess Cathleen* Stephen refuses to join the rioting nationalists; yet in *The Day of the Rabblement,* a pamphlet Joyce wrote in 1901, Yeats' theater is condemned for coming to terms with the rioters. Stephen takes care in his diary to dissociate himself from Yeats: "Michael Robartes remembers forgotten beauty and, when his arms wrap her round, he presses in his arms the loveliness which has long faded from the world. . . . I desire to press in my arms the loveliness which has not yet come into the world." Yeats was concerned with the traditional. Joyce, contemplating a break with Irish traditions, proposed new art. But as he remained obsessed with all else he had rejected, so he remained obsessed with Yeats, and echoes of that great poet are audible throughout Joyce's work. Except for his cynical interest in Lady Gregory and in A. E.'s Theosophy, this is Joyce's only connection with what he called the "cultic twalette." Perhaps, however, that literate Theosophical twilight helped save him from the directed light of the Jesuits. It is certain that the Jesuits, together with Aristotle and Aquinas, helped save him from the obscurities of the twilight. Defining Joyce's difference from the Anglo-Irish writers of the revival, Yeats' father saw Joyce as the "scholastic Irishman."

Too profoundly different from the Anglo-Irish to be welcome among them and too heretical for Catholics, Joyce was forced both out and in, out to exile and into himself. It was natural for him to become fascinated not only with home and religion but with himself in relation to them and often with himself alone. "Ourselves alone" was the slogan of Sinn Fein. Recognition of his distant kinship with those nationalists accounts for Joyce's continual reference to their name and motto.

Constituting a kind of Sinn Fein with a membership of one, Joyce was inevitably autobiographical. The first three stories of

Dubliners concern the early youth of Stephen Dedalus. The novel of his adolescence which followed these stories consists not only of *Stephen Hero* and *A Portrait of the Artist* but a great part of *Ulysses*. In all of these the central endowment of Stephen is pride. Lucifer, with whom he proudly identifies himself, fell from pride of the intellect. It is this cardinal sin that determines his conduct and demeanor, that causes his separation from others and prevents his return. His formal speech and impenetrable reserve keep his acquaintances at a distance, withering them with a vision of Byronic superiority and gloom. "You're a terrible man, Stevie," says Davin, "always alone." It is pride that causes Stephen to glory in and magnify his other sins. What the Church calls pride the world calls ego. "It was part of that ineradicable egoism which he was afterwards to call redeemer," says Joyce of Stephen, "that he conceived converging to him the deeds and thoughts of his microcosm." This sentence from *Stephen Hero* is a good description of *A Portrait of the Artist;* for in this book everything but Stephen is shadowy and unreal. The external world, dependent upon him, owes what existence it has to his scornful notice. In a technique which concentrates upon Stephen's impressions and his thoughts, Joyce found a suitable method for presenting an egoist. *Stephen Hero,* written before the discovery of this method, shows Stephen surrounded by real people and real things.

Stephen's equivalent in *Finnegans Wake* is described as "self exiled in upon his ego." Shem the Penman owes his name to Sir Charles Young's *Jim the Penman,* a Victorian drama about a forger, or else to a melodramatic novel of the same name by Dick Donovan. In this novel, Jim, who is born in Ireland, goes off to Paris to make forgery a "fine art." But society has its revenge, and he is transported into exile. A forger and a sham in the social eyes of Shaun the Post, Shem relives Joyce's career from the Berlitz School to the writing of *Ulysses,* his "farced epistol to the hibruws." This low character, whose improvidence and irresponsibility are distasteful to men of the middle class, annoys them further by telling family secrets, taking notes of private conversations, and publishing filth. "Anarch, egoarch, hiresiarch," says

Shaun to Shem, "you have reared your disunited kingdom on the vacuum of your own most intensely doubtful soul. Do you hold yourself then for some god in the manger, Shehohem, that you will neither serve nor let serve, pray nor let pray?" Sometimes Shem is Nick or the devil and sometimes he is Ipsey Secumbe or the supreme egoist. In the sixth, seventh, and ninth chapters of *Finnegans Wake,* where this self-portrait is presented, the tone is jocular as if Joyce were laughing not only at himself but at his reputation. Behind the jocularity, however, there seems to be considerable pain.

If, as some critics have claimed, there is also the enjoyment of self-pity behind this portrait and that of Stephen, then Joyce is sentimental. Rebecca West, who makes this charge in *Strange Necessity,* finds Joyce competent enough when he is writing about Mrs. Bloom, but narcissistic when writing about himself. Stephen seems to her an infantile dream of wish-fulfillment. That Joyce named his hero not only after Daedalus (surely a sign of pride) but after St. Stephen, the first martyr, seems to imply a compact of self-pity with self-love. Even the form taken by *A Portrait of the Artist,* that of the novel of adolescence, adds weight to this grievous charge.

Writers in this form invite the dangers of sentimentality. Few in our time have altogether escaped them. The defect of *The Way of All Flesh,* for example, is Samuel Butler's loving union with himself. Separated from an alien world, subject became one with object, and that distance which is necessary for art is nowhere to be found. A more recent example of the same defect, although somewhat redeemed by exuberance and apparent genius, is Thomas Wolfe's *Look Homeward, Angel.* These love affairs, which call for Rebecca West's rebuke, failed to get it.

In Joyce's autobiographical work the relation of subject to object or of the author to himself is different. Rebecca West's error is a confusion of Joyce with Stephen. As almost everybody knows, Joyce once said that the important words of his title are *as a Young Man.* From this remark and from a careful reading of the book it becomes evident that Joyce differs from Butler and

Wolfe in having an artist's detachment from what he is using. Stephen is not Joyce but Joyce's past. Stephen is sentimental; Joyce is not. In *A Portrait of the Artist as a Young Man,* the mature man looks back at his adolescent self, not to praise it, but to give it shape as an artist must. Stephen is Joyce's material. Like any artist Joyce was fascinated with his material, but as he wrote, he formalized and "distanced" it. By this process, which is that of all art, he composed the personal and gave it that symbolic form which, freed from the emotive and the personal, permits insight into reality.

Those who find a sentimental attachment in *A Portrait of the Artist* have failed to notice the tone. To his friend Frank Budgen, Joyce once said: " 'I haven't let this young man off very lightly, have I?' " A careful reading makes it apparent that Joyce is aloof and generally ironic in his treatment of Stephen. But Joyce's attitude is never explicit. Stephen is allowed to expose himself. Joyce limits his assistance to arranging contrasts and juxtapositions and to using a style which, following the contours of the hero's passion, becomes that passion while parodying it. His attitude toward Stephen is more obvious in *Ulysses* where that priggish hero is subjected to Mulligan's deflation and permitted to display his humorless egocentricity. Those who confuse Stephen with Joyce forget that Ibsen, Joyce's favorite, put ironic self-portraits into *The Master Builder* and *The Wild Duck,* and that he once remarked, "To be a poet is to preside over oneself as a judge." In his essay on Ibsen, Joyce praises the "angelic dispassionateness" of his author. This is Joyce's tribute to the detachment and symbolic projection he also achieved. It is possible that Joyce's Ibsenite *Exiles* is no less ironic than some of Ibsen's plays. If this is so, the hero is morbid and not the play.

The problem of Shem is somewhat more difficult. In this final self-portrait, although the materials are much the same as in the portrait of Stephen, the tone is different. The almost painful jocularity which takes the place of irony seems by its extravagance to conceal a personal involvement. There can be no doubt that Shem is more personal than Stephen. For one thing, Joyce resented the critics of *Ulysses;* and in *Finnegans Wake,* with almost impenetrable indirection, he took the opportunity of answering them. Allusions to Rebecca West, emerging throughout the book, accuse her of folly. That Joyce noticed her at all seems a descent from the proud eminence he had occupied and a betrayal of his impersonality. But as one reads the later chapters of *Finnegans Wake,* one finds that personal Shem, suffering his critics, takes his place in a vast impersonal structure and becomes one with his opposite. Personality is distanced again and symbolic form or art is revindicated.

In *A Portrait of the Artist* young Stephen raises these problems during the course of a discussion with Lynch. Art, says Stephen, is divided into three forms: the lyric, in which the artist presents his image in relation to himself; the epic, in which he presents his image in "mediate relation to himself and to others"; and the dramatic, in which he presents his image in relation to others. These three forms constitute a progression from the personal to the impersonal. Stephen continues:

> The simplest epical form is seen emerging out of lyrical literature when the artist prolongs and broods upon himself as the centre of an epical event and this form progresses till the centre of emotional gravity is equidistant from the artist himself and from others. The narrative is no longer purely personal. The personality of the artist passes into the narration itself, flowing round and round the persons and the action like a vital sea. This progress you will see easily in that old English ballad *Turpin Hero,* which begins in the first person and ends in the third person. The dramatic form is reached when the vitality which has flowed and eddied round each person fills every person with such vital force that he or she assumes a proper and intangible esthetic life. The personality of the artist, at first a cry or a cadence or a mood and then a fluid and lambent narrative, finally refines itself out of existence, impersonalizes itself, so to speak. The esthetic image in the dramatic form is life purified in and reprojected from the human imagination. The mystery of esthetic like that of material creation is accomplished. The

artist, like the God of the creation, remains within or behind or beyond or above his handiwork, invisible, refined out of existence, indifferent, paring his fingernails.

In *Finnegans Wake* this progression reappears symbolically as the course of the river Liffey: "the water of the livvying goes the way of all fish . . . to his moanolothe inturned." In other words, art or life progresses from the lyric condition of *The Way of All Flesh* to the dramatic condition of the interior monologue or of monolithic, unsentimental *Ulysses*. "In the future, the sister of the past," says the young Stephen of *Ulysses,* "I may see myself as I sit here now but by reflection from that which then I shall be." If we may take these declarations at their apparent value, we must conclude that it was Joyce's aim to be dramatic and godlike.

It has seemed odd to some critics that one who commends impersonality should write about himself. But, as we have seen, there is no paradox here. By aesthetic distance, the personal, becoming symbolic and formal, becomes dramatic. Fascinated with his personality, Joyce as artist is triumphantly aloof. His autobiographical works are evidence that the "lofty impersonal power" which he admired in Ibsen became his own.

During the discussion with Lynch, it becomes clear that for Stephen art has taken the place of religion and that the artist has taken the place of God. Earlier, however, Stephen has described the artist as "a priest of the eternal imagination." Whether as priest or god, the artist is divine, and all who speak of his creations must speak with reverence. Stephen, who has refused one priesthood in hope of another, assumes this tone as he explains the nature of the art he contemplates.

Art, says dedicated Stephen, is "the human disposition of sensible or intelligible matter for an esthetic end." A mountain is not art because it is not the human disposition of matter. An engine is not art because although it is the human disposition of matter, the matter is not disposed for an aesthetic end. For this definition and his other aesthetic ideas Stephen claims the authority of certain sentences from Aristotle and Aquinas. But his theory is less Aristotle than Aquinas, who, liberally interpreted and applied, is made to serve other ends than his own.

Aquinas says: " 'That is beautiful the apprehension of which pleases.' " Since the philosopher was also concerned with truth, Stephen finds it necessary to make a distinction. Truth is beheld by the intellect, which is appeased by the most satisfying relations of the intelligible; beauty is beheld by the imagination, appeased by the most satisfying relations of the sensible. Beyond good and evil, beauty is the formal relation of part to part in any aesthetic whole or of the parts to the whole. Distinguishing between good and bad art, Stephen finds that good or static art excites neither desire nor loathing. Bad or kinetic art, which excites desire or loathing, has two principal kinds: the pornographic and the didactic. The ideal stasis is called forth, prolonged, and dissolved by abstract formal relations. "That," says Lynch, "has the true scholastic stink."

In *Stephen Hero,* this theory, embodied in a paper, is read before the literary society at Stephen's college. Some of his more temperate auditors see danger in his scorn of instructive or elevating art. There is danger, they feel, in his conviction that the artist's only aim is the revelation of the beautiful at whatever cost to the proprieties, that the artist needs no sanction from house-holders, and that art is for the artist. Others, noting his secular application of doctrine, resent his "predisposition in favor of all but the premises of scholasticism." The President of the college defines Stephen's error. In emancipating the poet from all moral laws, he observes, Stephen is proposing art for art's sake.

That is precisely what Stephen is doing. Walter Pater and Oscar Wilde, the champions of art for art's sake, were among Joyce's authors. His paper before the University College Literary and Historical Society was delivered in 1900, the year Wilde, martyred by Philistines, died in exile. That the spell of Wilde's master was still alive in 1902 is shown by the Paterite prose of Joyce's undergraduate essay on the poet Mangan. Wilde's ideal of an art free from social, moral, and religious connections pleased the younger exile, but it pleased him more to make "monkish learning" serve Wilde's designs. Joyce differs from Wilde and Pater in that emphasis upon significant form in which he anticipated Clive Bell and Roger Fry, who, with some improvements, were to resume the cause of the nineties.

While in Paris, during his first exile, Joyce spent his days drinking cocoa, at times his only food, and reading Aristotle at the library of Sainte-Geneviève. That he subscribed at this period to the theory he attributed to Stephen is proved by the notebook which, after the manner of Coleridge, he kept in Paris and later on in Austria. In *A Portrait of the Artist* the theory is Stephen's manifesto, as at one time it was Joyce's, but there is no reason to suppose that it serves in *A Portrait of the Artist* as Joyce's manifesto. It is presented as the aesthetics of a young man. As such it has an important place in the pattern of the book. Joyce retained many of his early ideas, especially those on form, but he gave warmth to Stephen's cold abstractions by understanding and sympathy. If Joyce's early aesthetic theories are applied to the criticism of his later work, they must be applied with reservations. We must remember that mature Joyce was not young Stephen, nor was he a belated aesthete of the nineties.

The aesthetic theory is the climax of *A Portrait of the Artist*. After the discussion with Lynch, a mournful diminuendo takes us to the end where the accumulating tensions are dispersed, unresolved, among the fragments of Stephen's diary. Calling for aid upon Daedalus, his patron and model, Stephen is left hoping that physical exile in Paris will produce the great book he wants to write. The triumph of his break with home, religion, and Dublin is less real than he has supposed. There is no peace in his imagined country. He has dramatized himself as an artist at war with his surroundings, but, far from being an artist, he is little more than a lonesome, "morbidminded esthete." The gloom that is implicit throughout the last pages of the book is expressed in a dream recorded by Stephen in his diary. This vision of fabulous kings, set in stone, and of little men advancing from a cave down curving galleries of pillars must have been an actual nightmare. The symbols in their present context obviously refer to parents, home, religion, and country; the oppression charging the symbols is that of guilt. Guessing the significance of his dream, Joyce saw its value for his design. No conscious statement of the exile's

anxiety and guilt could be more effective. That the unsatisfying
diminuendo in which this dream takes its place was also inten-
tional is shown by the resumption and resolution of Stephen's conflicts in *Ulysses,* upon which *A Portrait of the Artist* leans for
support.

The story of how Stephen finally became an artist, how he
achieved the condition in which he could write *A Portrait of the
Artist,* how he came to unite personality with impersonality, and
how, finding his subject, he found himself constitutes an important theme of *Ulysses.*

At the beginning of this book Stephen is even gloomier than
at the end of *A Portrait of the Artist.* Called back from Paris by
the illness of his mother, he has nothing to show for the discom-
forts of exile. His guilt over leaving Church and home has been
intensified by his refusal to yield to his mother's dying request.
But an impious communion is beyond the capacity of this essential
Catholic. As he broods, plump Buck Mulligan, who has usurped
the home that belongs to Stephen, mocks him as he mocks
both home and Church. Mulligan is comfortably established.
Stephen, wearing castoff clothes, is manifestly disestablished.
While Stephen eats breakfast in the tower with Mulligan and
Haines, a visiting Englishman of the ruling class, a milkwoman
enters. To Stephen she is the Poor Old Woman, Ireland's symbol,
as Haines is symbol of Ireland's imperial master. Stephen's immediate problem is to get money, preferably by writing—but from
whom? From Haines or the milkwoman? He sees no hope of an
audience in either. Moreover, as Mulligan implies, the great book
Stephen has promised within ten years remains to be written.
Against these thoughts, scornful silence and arrogance are no
defense.

In the second chapter of *Ulysses,* while Stephen is teaching
in Mr. Deasy's academy, these troubles find a symbolic expression
which is somewhat less direct. Pyrrhus is the subject of the history
lesson. One of the students makes the inevitable quotation:
" 'Another victory like that and we are done for.' " Pyrrhus occurs
at this point not because he happens to be the assigned subject
for June 16, 1904, but because he and his kind of victory are

symbols for Stephen's condition. The victory Stephen has prematurely celebrated at the end of *A Portrait of the Artist* seems Pyrrhic now. Another such empty triumph and he is done for. This seemingly casual projection of his feeling is intensified by what follows. After one of his students has confused Pyrrhus with a pier, Stephen defines a pier as "a disappointed bridge." This rich symbol of frustration refers to exile, unity of being, and art.

Stephen's bitterness finds fresh embodiment during the lesson on literature. In Milton's lament for Edward King, sunk beneath the Irish Sea, Stephen discovers his own elegy and his mother's, and for a moment he entertains Milton's hope of resurrection. But by his riddle of the fox burying his grandmother under a hollybush Stephen deflates this fancy. He himself is the too cunning fox. The buried grandmother is at once his mother, the Church, and the Poor Old Woman. A tree of life, the hollybush represents the resurrection for which Stephen hopes while professing disbelief. Later in the hour, during a conversation with Mr. Deasy, Stephen says, "History is a nightmare from which I am trying to awake." History or the oppressive tradition of Church, nation, and home is what the fox has been trying to bury and revive. Unaware of his own profound traditionalism, Stephen feels only the burden of the past.

The scene in the National Library shows Stephen's imprudence and uneasiness among the established. A. E. and John Eglinton, representing the Anglo-Irish literary movement, compose his audience. As Stephen shows off before them, he shows them up. Within himself he sneers at their nationalism and Theosophy—at all, in fact, that is enjoying the success he wants. His contempt, however silent, is unconcealed. A. E. has his revenge. He is about to publish an anthology of young poets, from whose number Stephen has been carefully excluded. Not a member of the gang in power or of any gang, he does not belong. There will be a gathering at George Moore's that night. Stephen is not invited. Filled with the sense of the exclusion he has provoked, he is talking eloquently of Shakespeare's exile and of his usurping brother, when Mulligan, Stephen's "usurper," enters.

By his wit Mulligan punctures Stephen's pretensions, and success remains with the successful.

This new deflation reminds Stephen of his Cretan example: "Fabulous artificer, the hawklike man," he says to himself. "You flew. Whereto? Newhaven-Dieppe, steerage passenger. Paris and back. Lapwing. Icarus. *Pater, ait*. Seabedabbled, fallen, weltering. Lapwing you are. Lapwing he." Stephen finds himself less Daedalus now than Icarus. Not only the image of Icarus but the word "lapwing" carries his irony and despair. The name of this bird combines Anglo-Saxon words for leap and fall.

Lapwing Icarus will do as an image for his estate, but a juster comparison would have been with Narcissus. Not Stephen but Joyce establishes this less flattering analogy. On his table at 7 Eccles Street, Mr. Bloom keeps a statue of Narcissus, which he has picked up during his wanderings as on that day he is to pick up Stephen. In another book the possession of such an object would be accidental and insignificant, but nothing is accidental or insignificant in *Ulysses*. Losing the actual Stephen, Mr. Bloom keeps Stephen's image. The trouble with Stephen is the self-centered innocence that Mr. Bloom finds attractive. Like narcissistic Isabel in *Finnegans Wake,* Stephen sits before a mirror, lost in wonder. However developed his intellect and imagination, he is emotionally immature. Besides showing up A. E. and Eglinton, he has exposed himself.

Stephen's ego leads not only to a social difficulty but to an aesthetic difficulty as well. Because the ego is not enough for the artist to work with, Stephen finds himself sterile. The artist needs something greater than self and outside it. The detachment so necessary for art needs to be balanced by some attachment. The artist needs total reality, both inner and outer, together with understanding and sympathy, and a relationship between himself and other things. Even the autobiographical writer needs these things in order to know himself; for egocentricity is not self-knowledge. Equipped with a fine theory of how to say something, Stephen has nothing to say.

Joyce symbolized Stephen's simultaneous discovery of reality and self by the meeting between Stephen and Mr. Bloom. Their meeting is parallel to the reconciliation of Dolph or Shem with Kev or Shaun at the end of the tenth chapter of *Finnegans Wake*. Shem, the exile, comes to terms with the world as represented by Shaun. Self-pity and self-love and all the insolence of pride yield to mature acceptance, without resentment, of what Freud calls the reality principle. "Let us be singulfied," says Shem to his worldly opposite. These meetings of Stephen and Bloom or of Shem and Shaun are not autobiographical in the sense that Joyce met a Jew on June 16, 1904, or accepted a brother, but they are true to his experience. Whether it was during his starvation in Paris, or during his difficulties in Trieste, or even in Dublin before he sailed, Joyce encountered reality. A man with a wife and children and no money to support them cannot remain apart from it. Mr. Bloom is the symbol of that reality.

But Mr. Bloom, more than a symbol of that, also symbolizes the father. In *A Portrait of the Artist* Stephen abandons his earthly and his heavenly fathers. But having lost them, he wants them back. Mulligan calls him "Japhet in search of a father." *Ulysses* takes the form of a quest, and Japhet, the quester, is almost everybody.

Almost everybody, in recent literature that is, has undertaken such a quest. At a time of uncertainty and doubt when many men of sensibility have lost God and with Him their values and their sense of connection with things, one might expect a search for something to take the place of what is lost, for something outside the self and larger than the self to depend on. Whether it have as its object tradition or what some call integration, the life force or the five-year plan, the latest yogi from Los Angeles or Almighty God, the search is the same and so is its real object. Such a quest has occupied Bernard Shaw, Aldous Huxley, T. S. Eliot, and innumerable others, big and small. Each has undertaken under one name or another what Joyce symbolized as the hunt for the father. With his own loss and need in mind he made a suggestive image, perhaps the most adequate of all, for the central occupation of modern man.

The power of this image is shown by its effect upon Virginia Woolf. In *To the Lighthouse,* published five years after *Ulysses,* she presents a double quest, that of intellectual Mr. Ramsay for the absolute and that of Mrs. Ramsay, a woman of great wisdom, for eternity and peace. As he tries to transcend the limits of the intellect, she tries to transcend the limits of time. Their quest ends at last with Mr. Ramsay's arrival at the lighthouse. This lonely tower with its triple beam and stark design represents God the Father, eternal and absolute. Mrs. Woolf's lighthouse owes much to Mr. Bloom; but Joyce had provided an even closer model in *Dubliners*. "An Encounter," the second story of that collection, is an epitome of *Ulysses*. Here too the swarming streets of Dublin are threaded by a symbolic quest. Three boys, playing hookey, plan an adventure. Leo Dillon, who, since he is to be a priest and has a Father, fails to appear; so Stephen and Mahony set out by themselves. Their goal is the Pigeon House—successively a fort, a lighthouse, and a power station—on its lonely breakwater out in the bay. On their way they encounter an elderly pervert, who, frustrating their quest for power, light, and Pigeon, may be an ironic embodiment of what questers may expect. The story might have been called Toward the Pigeon House.

Bloom is not the disappointment of a quest, but the father found. *Ulysses* commences with Stephen's mother. In the first chapter, however, the theme of paternity is introduced and the quest suggested. During his walk along Sandymount beach, Stephen thinks about the consubstantiality or oneness of Father and Son while Mr. Bloom, on the way to the cemetery, is thinking of his father, his dead son, and Stephen's abandoned father. Mr. Bloom wants a son and Stephen a father. These preliminaries lead to the scene in the library, in which Stephen, indulging his obsession with families, discusses *Hamlet,* an excellent focus for thoughts of father and son and a parallel for the future relationship of Stephen, Bloom, and Mrs. Bloom. "Fatherhood," says Stephen, "is a mystical estate." Bloom passes through the library and out the door. The way has now been prepared for the "atonement" of Stephen with his mystical father. They finally meet at the maternity hospital that night and remain together until the early morning. Although invited to stay at Bloom's home, Stephen departs. But the encounter with Bloom has changed Stephen's inhumanity to humanity. The egoist has discovered charity, the greatest of virtues, and compassion for mankind. In his essay on Mangan, Joyce finds the aim of literature to be the praise of life, and in the essay on Ibsen he admires the poet's pity for men. "Pity," Stephen says in *A Portrait of the Artist,* "is the feeling which arrests the mind in the presence of whatsoever is grave and constant in human sufferings and unites it with the human sufferer." He now discovers what this means, and, leaving Bloom, he goes away to write *Ulysses.*

Bloom the father, who has introduced Stephen to man, symbolizes man. He is ill-informed, common, and victim of all our habitual failings. On the other hand, he has many of our virtues— kindliness, sympathy, and courage. He is, in short, domestic man. Yet during the course of *Ulysses* he is identified with Moses, Elijah, Jesus, and God. This must be looked into.

The newspaper-office episode, in which Stephen and Bloom separately encounter journalists, lawyers, and wits, has Moses as a central theme. The quotations and allusions which carry this burden culminate in Stephen's parable of the plums or "A Pisgah Sight of Palestine." The reference to Bloom is unmistakable. He is one who will lead Stephen to the promised land without getting there himself. Bloom's prophetical function is confirmed by John Alexander Dowie, the American evangelist, whose handbill, announcing the coming of Elijah, seems to be everywhere. Ignorant of its meaning, Mr. Bloom throws his copy away, but as it floats down the Liffey, it assumes an importance equal to that of Father Conmee and the Lord Lieutenant General. Like them, it is one of the clues that thread the labyrinth of Dublin. What the handbill announces is the ascent of ben Bloom Elijah to the glory of the brightness in a chariot of fire. This ascension, which anticipates a more glorious one, occurs at the end of the scene in Barney Kiernan's pub. It is in this chapter that Bloom has begun to assume the attributes of crucified Christ. That the favorite oath of the nameless narrator is "Jesus" is not without meaning. Bloom is likened to a sheep (the paschal lamb), and in his agony he proclaims that, like himself, Christ and God are Jews. But these and countless other allusions throughout the book do not mean

that Bloom is either prophet or God. In discovering Bloom or
mankind, Stephen finds something to take the place of God. God
is a metaphor for man.

In the brothel scene, a soldier calls Stephen a parson, and a
whore calls him a "spoiled priest." Neither of these terms is
altogether inappropriate; for, emerging in this scene as the priest
of man, he celebrates a Mass for his metaphorical divinity. Enter-
ing nighttown, he chants what Joyce calls the *Introit* for paschal
time and after that distorts the *Iudica me.* These preliminaries
suggest that the chapter is a kind of Mass for Easter time or, since
it is past the middle of June, for another resurrection. This Mass
is opposite to the Black Mass celebrated by Mulligan and Haines
somewhat later in the chapter. Whereas they celebrate death and
the devil, Stephen celebrates human life. Mr. Bloom, to whom
Stephen's Mass is offered, passes rapidly through the conditions
of Moses and Elijah to that of Christ, and, because of the oneness
of Father and Son, to that of God. As Messiah, he builds the
"new Bloomusalem," and after performing miracles of loaves and
fishes, becomes the "scape-goat." During this sacrifice, the Daugh-
ters of Erin recite his litany. His assertion of human dignity
against the enchantments of Bella Cohen is the resurrection.

Allusions to light—transformed at one point by Bloom's
kidney fixation to "Bright's! Lights!"—culminate appropriately
in Stephen's destruction of the chandelier. It is necessary to put
out the old light before turning on the new. It is necessary to
destroy God the thunderer or, as Stephen calls him, the "shout in
the street," before coming to terms with man, another shout in
the street. The destruction of the chandelier is preceded by an
Apocalypse. To the tune of "The Holy City," Elijah Dowie,
evangelically intruding upon the Romish scene, announces the
end of the world. His sermon identifies the congregation with
Christ, not only Stephen and Bloom, but Lynch and all the
whores. According to Dowie—and in the present context we have
every reason to believe him—everyman is Christ.

The moment of Stephen's enlightenment follows the Apocalypse. "I flew. My foes beneath me. And ever shall be. World
without end. (He cries.) *Pater!* Free!" Flight is associated not

only with Daedalus but, because of a dream Stephen has had the night before, with Bloom. *Pater* has reference to Stephen's earthly father, God, and Bloom. World without end is a vision of the cycles that are one day to support Stephen's humanity. Neither this vision nor the smashing of the light marks his atonement with Bloom. That does not happen until they have arrived at 7 Eccles Street.

But the sacrifice has been celebrated. As in *Finnegans Wake,* the Mass is presented here not so much by parody as by allusion to some of its parts. Acts of self-surrender precede acts of love. A kind of transubstantiation has taken place and communion approaches. In fact, since *Ulysses* begins with the beginning of the Mass, the entire book may be considered a symbolic celebration of Stephen's communion with man.

As Bloom and Stephen leave the brothel, Bloom feels fatherly. Others "in quest of paternity" have come to him, and, Father-Son, he recognizes Stephen as the questing son. But in his social capacity Bloom sees Stephen as a scholar who will bring credit to the house of Bloom. Fatherly, hopeful Bloom takes Stephen to the cabman's shelter, where he offers him a bun and a cup of coffee. Refusing the bun, Stephen sips the coffee before shoving it aside. Although he unenthusiastically recognizes Bloom as "Christus," he is still reluctant to take the proffered communion. But by the time they sit down amicably together in the kitchen at 7 Eccles Street, Stephen is ready. Bloom prepares two cups of Epps's cocoa. Host and guest drink "Epps's massproduct" in "jocoserious" silence. "Massproduct," the key word, means three things: the cocoa is mass-produced for the trade; as the product of a symbolic Mass, it is the sacrament; and it suggests the masses for whom it is produced. The drinking of this cocoa, Stephen's communion with man, is the climax of the hunt for the father. Cocoa must have been a personal symbol for coming to terms with man and external reality. It was perhaps while living on cocoa in Paris that Joyce began to understand the world around him.

The sacrament of humanity is unaccompanied by a bun, but since either element of the Eucharist includes the other, the general outline is clear. The Mass is done. Stephen, having found what he wants, goes. Bloom holds a candle, and Stephen, holding his "diaconal" hat, chants the 113th Psalm, sung at Vespers. Bloom's candle appears to be the paschal candle, lighted on Holy Saturday to symbolize the resurrection and the renewal of light. If this is so, Stephen's destruction of the chandelier, acquiring additional significance, becomes the Tenebrae or the extinguishing of candles on Holy Thursday to symbolize the death of God.

As they stand together in the back yard, they see a celestial sign. "A star precipitated with great apparent velocity across the firmament from Vega in the Lyre above the zenith beyond the stargroup of the Tress of Berenice towards the zodiacal sign of Leo." In this sign is the summary of Stephen's career. Vega means falling; Berenice is a mother killed by her son; Lyra implies the lyrical or the self-centered; and Leo is Leopold Bloom or mankind. Brilliant Stephen abandons egocentricity and mother-fixation for reconciliation with the father and with humanity. Every chapter of *Ulysses* has its symbol. The symbol of this chapter, according to Joyce, is "comets." Stephen is a meteor, but Bloom is a comet, ever departing and returning, in a regular orbit.

It should be plain by now that much of the meaning of *Ulysses* is conveyed indirectly by means of parallel, allusion, and symbol. Of the many symbols that carry Stephen's acceptance of reality, water is one of the most important. Water means reality. In *A Portrait of the Artist* Stephen enjoys his aesthetic rapture by the sea. But instead of going swimming, he rolls up his trousers, like J. Alfred Prufrock, and goes wading. *Ulysses* finds him still afraid to enter reality. In the first chapter the sea is maternal and dangerous. In the third, after having refused to swim, he prudently walks along the beach. Later in the book, he is described as "hydrophobe." The month is June and he has not had a bath since the previous October. But when he goes to encounter reality in the brothel, he chants *Vidi aquam,* the *Asperges* of the Mass for paschal time. He understands at last the meaning of water; for, as Carl Jung says, "The way of the soul in search of its lost father leads to the water." Although Stephen refuses to wash his hands in the house of Bloom as he refuses at first to take the proffered sacrament, he goes out to celebrate the river Liffey and her ultimate union with the paternal sea.

Whether paternal or maternal, the sea fascinated Joyce. His friends tell us how he loved to sit beside it, listening to the wavespeech, or beside the river Loire. When he died, they say, he was planning an epic about the sea.

In a sense, Stephen's discovery of what is around him is not so much the discovery of something external to himself as of something within himself. Discovering the humanity of Bloom, he discovers his own humanity. The scene in the National Library shows him aware of this as he is aware of much else that he does not yet understand. Shakespeare, he says, is all his characters; for to a man of genius, his own image is the standard of all experience. Quoting Maeterlinck, Stephen adds, " 'If Socrates leave his house today he will find the sage seated on his doorstep.' We walk through ourselves . . . always meeting ourselves." In the brothel, thinking at the piano of the symbolic octave, Stephen enigmatically remarks: "What went forth to the ends of the world to traverse not itself. God, the sun, Shakespeare, a commercial traveller, having itself traversed in reality itself becomes that self." Bloom, who is at once a commercial traveller, a substitute for God, and one of Shakespeare's parallels, is not external to Stephen, but rather is the recognition by Stephen of what he has in common with other men. Stephen is the recognition by Joyce of how he differs from other men. However different Bloom and Stephen seem to be, Bloom is aware of an "analogy" between them. Stephen's simultaneous recognition of this analogy is what changes him from "potential poet" to poet. Because of Bloom, the Joyce who wrote *Ulysses* is closer to Bloom than to Stephen.

It is curious that the artist exiled from society should find his center and himself in common man. But Joyce's artistic need led him to the society he had renounced. It was his destined and necessary subject, and the artist must come to terms with his subject. But as he approached society and man, Joyce began to complicate his manner of writing as if to compensate for that approach. His difficulty increased his distance from man as his sympathy decreased it. The new attachment required a new detachment, and, with the acceptance of humanity, the preservation of self.

Having identified himself with everyman, yet having preserved his independence, Joyce could create Stephen or Bloom or, what is harder, Mrs. Bloom. Daedalus at last, he could place them in a suitable labyrinth and fly above it. *Finnegans Wake,* occupied by Earwicker and Anna Liffey, is a "nightmaze."

CHAPTER TWO

HUMANITY

THE humanity contemplated by Joyce was at once his own and everyman's. With the aid of his new understanding he explored all levels of reality, inner and outer, particular and universal, and the special provinces of day and night. As *Finnegans Wake* is the total reality of night, *Ulysses* is the total reality of day.

Joyce's vision of day is embodied in three characters, Stephen Dedalus, Leopold Bloom, and Molly Bloom, whose initials head the three main divisions of the book. The first division begins with S for Stephen, the second with M for Molly, and the third with P for Poldy. Whereas Molly and Poldy represent being, Stephen represents becoming. By assimilating them, he achieves their condition, but this triumph, merely suggested in the text, occurs off stage, and the book before us is the principal evidence that it has occurred.

Mr. Bloom, a solid and finally an enormous creature, is composed of contradictions. He is practical and impractical, hopeful and resigned, prudent and imprudent, faithful and un- faithful, decent and indecent, meek and pushing; for he is every- man. Not only our general image, he is the image of the citizen of cities. But he is also a particular man with a life of his own and with concerns peculiar to himself.

The first two chapters in which he appears are devoted to establishing his character. Like most citizens, he is interested in science and business. As he walks the streets, his mind is occupied with the laws of physics. A common education assures him that 32 feet per second has something to do with falling bodies. In mourning clothes for the funeral, he wonders whether black conducts or reflects (refracts is it?) heat; he admires the invention of the telescope by Edison or Galileo; and he is bothered all day by the enigma of parallax. As he walks the streets, his mind also turns upon the possibilities of business. Passing a pub, he automatically computes the number of barrels consumed per year and the profit to publican and brewer. He thinks of ingenious devices for advertising stationery or trousers. He plans a tramway to the cattle market. But his commercial shrewdness is no more practical than his knowledge of science. Through imprudence and what might be called the poetry of commerce he has lost each of his jobs as he will certainly lose his present job of advertising-canvasser.

In this capacity he embodies the central concern of the middle class, which venerates production less than publicity. His social and political ideas compose a bourgeois Utopia. In the next to the last chapter his daydream of commercial success and of a house in the suburbs fixes an ideal of "tepid security." Here he will enjoy a mortgage, an encyclopedia, and a lawn mower.

In Bloom's first two chapters his interest in women, their parts and their dress, is established. There is, for example, his interrupted view of silken legs as the lady ascends the jaunting car in front of the Grosvenor, and in a later chapter there is his more satisfactory view of Gerty MacDowell's exhibition on the beach as she leans back to watch the Roman candles. This interest in underthings, especially drawers, is partly a result of frustration. From the same cause come his infantile pleasure at stool and the fantasies that interrupt his lively concern with external things. These interests and pleasures are substitutes for his wife, who has substituted other objects for him. His frustration, however, is not only marital but social. His sociable instincts are constantly rebuffed, and his position in Dublin is no better than his position at 7 Eccles Street. Having left home that morning without a key, he spends the day searching for crossed keys, which, on the literal level, are to serve as an advertisement for the house of Keyes, and

on the symbolic level, represent the wholeness he desires. Crossed
keys are a symbol of the Isle of Man. It may seem odd that
Bloom, Stephen's symbol of humanity and completeness, should
himself be in search of completeness. But compared to Stephen,
he seems complete. Whereas Stephen is only a son as yet, Bloom
is son, father, husband, cuckold, and friend. However infantile
and perverse at times, he is comparatively mature and much more
widely experienced. If he were perfect in anything, he would
cease to represent mankind. To Joyce's way of thinking, not even
Jesus, with whom Bloom is compared, approaches the humanity
of Bloom. Jesus was a bachelor, and, as Joyce once said, living
with a woman is the hardest thing a man can do.

Bloom resembles Jesus, however, in benevolence and charity.
Although Bloom's tenderness toward Stephen is complicated by
self-interest, his sympathy with Mrs. Breen and with the survivors
of Paddy Dignam is unqualified. Pity and concern lead him to
the maternity hospital where Mrs. Purefoy is in labor. These
human qualities distinguish Bloom from the impious medical
students. He alone at the riotous party is a father; and fatherhood
has given him reverence for life. This is what Stephen still lacks.
He notices the seagulls, but Mr. Bloom feeds them. At his hallu-
cinatory trial in the brothel, the gulls, appearing as witnesses for
the defense, cry "Kaw kave kankury kake," which in the speech
of gulls means: he gave Banbury cake.

Joyce made this generous man a Jew for several reasons.
Jesus was a Jew. Today the Jew is both typical citizen and exiled
wanderer. Seeing in the Jew a symbol for himself, Joyce projected
Bloom. Attached by understanding and detached by art, Joyce
presented Bloom with irony and compassion. He is at once a
comic and a pathetic figure. But he emerges heroically in the end
as one of the greatest representatives of human dignity.

Bloom's patience, courage, and freedom from self-pity are
admirably displayed at Barney Kiernan's pub. But his real triumph is his attitude toward Mrs. Bloom, whose infidelity he
suffers for a number of reasons. Something of a masochist, he
likes to suffer. His fatalism and perversity recommend inaction.
But these negative impulses are balanced by his wife's attractive-

ness. After sixteen years he is still drawn to her, and all the day she fills his thoughts. He needs her not only for support but, as we have seen, for the contact she provides with other men. From this tension comes that equanimity which is the climax of *Ulysses*. All complexities of day are peacefully resolved.

Meanwhile Mrs. Bloom lies in bed where she belongs. Beyond good and evil, she thinks of life and love. She thinks of breast, thigh, and bottom, of Blazes Boylan, the latest of her lovers, and of other men. The reference of the pronoun "he" is almost never clear as her mind, embracing men, confuses them with one another. Thinking of Stephen as a possible lover, she decides to read a book that she may be attractive to one who is almost a professor and a poet. She thinks of Bloom. Although she sees through him as she sees through every man, she is puzzled by something in him that escapes her and demands her admiration. As she complains about Bloom while accepting him, so she complains about woman's lot while enjoying it. A realist, she accepts everything but the indecencies of Rabelais. As for intellect, she has none, but she is not without intelligence and wit. It is she who describes the singer Ben Dollard as a "base barreltone."

There are masculine elements in most women, but none in Mrs. Bloom. Like the cat, with which Joyce compares her, she has been created out of feminine elements. She is not everywoman but the essential being of everywoman. As fundamental and symbolic as her cat, she appears as "Gea-Tellus" or earth-earth, "fulfilled, recumbent, big with seed." By its redundancy this name expresses her meaning. Larger than individual Mrs. Bloom and far older, she is the Great Mother of the ancients. Her voice, the voice of the flesh, is endlessly affirmative. Her monologue which begins with "Yes," and uses "yes" as its refrain, suitably ends with "Yes." From its immediate reference to Bloom, this final word is raised by the chapter that precedes it and by the book that it ends to a general affirmation. The last two pages of her monologue and of the book are a hymn to God and nature. The center of natural life, she praises it.

Bloom's equanimity resolves his private tensions. By her existence and her position at the end Mrs. Bloom resolves the tensions of the book. She makes the worries and frustrations of Bloom seem irrelevant and the problems of Stephen peripheral. Compared to her, nothing seems very important. By her irrationality she reconciles all rational conflicts. Stephen and Bloom, conflicting opposites, become one in her. As she thinks of them, their differences fall away to leave them united in a common being. She is the agent of reconcilation and its symbol.

That she served Joyce in this capacity is evident. In *A Portrait of the Artist*, Stephen, indifferent to fatherhood, is devoted to the Virgin Mary, who is connected in his mind with his mother. In the library scene of *Ulysses,* beginning to understand the father, Stephen attacks the cult of Mary as something thrown to the mob of Europe. But as he substitutes Bloom for God and earthly father, so Joyce substituted Mrs. Bloom for the Virgin and his earthly mother. As Stephen discovers humanity in Bloom, so Joyce, going beyond Stephen, discovered life itself in Mrs. Bloom. The realization of Mrs. Bloom must have had the effect of what Jung calls the reconciling symbol. Through it Joyce united Bloom with Stephen or one side of his own nature with the other. The final s of Mrs. Bloom's acceptance, meeting the initial S of the first chapter, leads us in a circle to Stephen again and back to Mr. Bloom.

All the women of *Ulysses* are aspects of Mrs. Bloom. Milly, her daughter, and Gerty MacDowell, on the beach, represent her girlhood. Mrs. Breen is Mrs. Bloom's possible, although unlikely, frustration; and Mrs. Purefoy in her hospital is Mrs. Bloom's possible fruition. Mrs. Purefoy, far more specialized than Mrs. Bloom, is there to represent the fertility of Mother Earth. As goddess of fertility, Mrs. Bloom serves Joyce in still another way. She is not only the reconciling symbol but the symbol of the artist's creative mind. At the maternity hospital, while Mrs. Purefoy is multiplying, Stephen is speaking of the Virgin Mary and of Yeats' rose, another feminine symbol of reconciliation. "In woman's womb," he says, "word is made flesh but in the spirit of the maker all flesh that passes becomes the word that shall not pass away." The word is the male or intellectual principle; the womb is the artist's creative power or the feminine element within him. As the word must fertilize the womb, so the womb must create the word. In this capacity, Mrs. Bloom, a projection of Joyce's essential being, is no more external to him than Stephen, the intellectual principle, or Bloom, the word made flesh.

As a character in *Ulysses,* Mrs. Bloom is also the word made flesh. It is as a person in a story, and not as a many-leveled symbol, that she must appeal to the common reader. Few feminine characters in literature are as convincing as she or the result of such humor and terrible clarity of vision. Chaucer's Wife of Bath, though more sketchily presented, is comparable. *Man and Superman* proves that Shaw had the humor and insight of Chaucer and Joyce if not their capacity to dramatize a vision. But Ann's curtain speech is Mrs. Bloom's monologue reduced to a sentence. Goethe's "eternal womanly" comes to mind together with Virginia Woolf's Mrs. Ramsay, who, although more limited than these other creations, has the authentic quality. Almost alone among women, Virginia Woolf, her eye perhaps on Mrs. Bloom, created an essential woman. D. H. Lawrence, good at relationships between people, was too feminine to succeed in establishing their characters. It is notable that *Ulysses* disgusted him as the work of Rabelais disgusted Mrs. Bloom. If we compare her with her predecessors and contemporaries, we must place her alongside the Wife of Bath. Nowhere is Joyce's understanding more apparent and nowhere his mixture of humor, irony, and compassion. Mrs. Bloom is a triumph of that static art of which Stephen dreamed. Fully created, she invites neither desire nor loathing but contemplation alone. Her final "Yes" is ours as, affirming life and art, it was Joyce's too.

If we take Mrs. Bloom and Stephen and combine them with Mr. Bloom, we compose something like ideal man. Mrs. Bloom is his feminine flesh, Stephen his male intellect and imagination, and Mr. Bloom all that lies between these extremes. That the ideal figure will be closer to Mr. Bloom than to the others is a tribute to his humanity.

This trinity is surrounded by many people who support or help compose Joyce's vision of man and the world. *Ulysses* resembles the novels of Dickens and the plays of Shakespeare in wealth of minor characters. Rarely described, they exist dramatically by their speech and by their relations with others. Their presentation differs in kind from sketch to portrait. Blazes Boylan, a caricature, who lives by fleshly mechanics, is a figure of fun. Simon Dedalus, Stephen's discarded father, exists by song and wit. The sky, this agreeable man observes, looking from the carriage window, is "as uncertain as a child's bottom." The nameless narrator of Mr. Bloom's experience with the one-eyed Citizen is one of the most complex and suggestive portraits of the book although we never see him. Almost all the characters of *Dubliners* and some from *A Portrait of the Artist* reappear in *Ulysses*. There are, for example, Lenehan, Corley, Martin Cunningham, Joe Hynes, Father Conmee, Dixon, and Lynch. Their functions are various, but all these Dubliners help create their city and trace the pattern of the day.

They also have a part in Joyce's composition of man's fundamental experience. *Ulysses* presents love, hate, eating, digesting, and excreting, birth, death, and sleep. It presents the relations of man and woman, parents and children, man and society, man and art, man and the universe. The visit to the maternity hospital is balanced by the trip to the graveyard. This chapter of tombs is preceded by another chapter of wombs, the fifth chapter of the book, in which Mr. Bloom calls for his mail and buys the soap. The atmosphere is sleepy; the mood suggests escape. All the symbolism of flowers, churches, and valises is maternal; and Bloom's bathtub at the end of the chapter becomes "a womb of warmth." The rhymes of Stephen's poem, in the newspaper office, are tomb-womb. It will be recalled that in *A Portrait of the Artist,* Temple finds the truth of life in this sentence from a zoology book: " 'Reproduction is the beginning of death.' " Stephen is not yet ready to receive from the lips of a fool this statement of what was to become his preoccupation and that of Dylan Thomas.

Joyce told his friend Frank Budgen that he was more concerned with Bloom than with the techniques for presenting him. Coming from an artist as conscious of his art as Joyce this statement seems odd. But even the most conscious artist may regard his method as no more than a means to the end of creating an object or of exploring its nature. When we look at Dürer's rabbit, if we have read Clive Bell, we may think of essential form. But it is likely that Dürer's conscious mind was occupied with rabbit as his hand and eye and total being attended to the form, automatically solving the problems of line, mass, and texture. An artist's way of doing a thing is his way of knowing it, and, in a sense, his way of doing it is what he does. Whatever he may say, he knows that he cannot separate his object from technique and form. If we separate them for analysis, we must put them together again or, if that is impossible, think about how they were before we started.

Mr. Bloom owes his solidity to the techniques that compose him. Through them we see him inside and out and from every point of view. We know him better than anyone else in fiction and far better than we know our friends. He is as three-dimensional as sculpture yet as suggestive as poetry. Maybe his search for the meaning of parallax is Joyce's clue to what gives Bloom ambiguity and dimension. Parallax is the apparent displacement of an object by an actual change in the point of view from which it is seen. On one level at least Bloom's parallax is Joyce's technique, or, if we refuse to separate object from technique, Bloom himself is parallax. Joyce used many points of view to place and displace his characters. For inner, daytime reality he used impressionism, the stream of consciousness, and a variety of other methods, each of them adapted to object, time, and circumstance.

The first three stories of *Dubliners* and *A Portrait of the Artist* are presented impressionistically through the consciousness of Stephen, who is made to seem both subject and object. No method could be more appropriate for the creation of an egoist. Matter and method become identical. Telling his story in third person, the author looks into the head of his central character or observer and records the contents of that head. The author sees external reality only through his observer's eyes, but, since he himself is telling the story, he can select what he wants and ignore the rest. The observer's impressions, selected, arranged, and sometimes commented upon by the author, constitute reality. In *A Portrait of the Artist* we look through Joyce's eyes, looking through the eyes of Stephen, as he looks at himself or sometimes at other things. Our looking is confined to important moments. The time is commonly the present, but through memory the observer's mind may also explore the past, or, departing from time, his mind may form abstractions. As Stephen sits in the algebra class, his mind, partly occupied with the unfolding equations, ranges from Shelley, sin, and the Blessed Virgin to events of yesterday or the day before. Through memory and thought the moment acquires levels, meanings, and dimensions.

The subjective techniques of *Ulysses* are more formidable. Of these the stream of consciousness or the interior monologue is most striking. More dramatic and immediate than impressionism and apparently less selective, this method covers a greater area of reality and all its levels. The author seems to have been refined away, as he sits apart, godlike, paring his fingernails and contemplating his creation. No longer looking through his eyes into the observer's mind, we occupy that mind. Its total contents of thought, sensation, and memory pass through us. Thought is by image as well as word, and the tone of experience is neither verbal nor imagistic. The author must not only record his observer's verbalized thought but, since books consist of words, must verbalize what his observer feels. Without seeming to select from that confusion of thought and feeling that constitutes our experience, the author must select what defines character, advances the plot, and establishes the interconnections and the relationships of part to part by which the novel becomes a formal pattern. By interference of this kind he serves the causes of realism and art.

Joyce said that he discovered the interior monologue in *Les Lauriers sont coupés* (1888) by Edouard Dujardin, a forgotten symbolist. What Joyce got from Dujardin's novel was a hint rather than a method. The development of the interior monologue was Joyce's accomplishment. As the blank verse of the early Elizabethans was transformed into something new by Shakespeare, so in Joyce's hands Dujardin's wooden invention became flexible and poetic. Joyce could have found hints in other places, in Hamlet's soliloquy, for example, or in the speech

of Mr. Jingle. The philosophers too were discovering reality in
the flow of experience. In 1890 William James described and
named the stream of consciousness. A few years later Bergson
found the absolute in psychological duration, which is the stream
under a different name. Interest in subjective flux was general
while Joyce was writing *Ulysses*. Thoroughly well-read, he was
aware of this interest, whether literary or philosophical; and he
was not alone in making use of flux. While Joyce was writing
Ulysses, Proust was arranging memories in France, and in England, Dorothy Richardson, developing the subjective methods of
Henry James and Conrad, was floating down a private stream.
Virginia Woolf's stream of consciousness flows from Joyce and
Bergson. But for all her characters, male or female, young or
old, at any time or place, her stream is the same. Joyce differs
from his most eminent imitator in being able to regulate the
stream.

    Stephen's monologue differs entirely from Bloom's, and Mrs.
Bloom's differs from both. During Stephen's walk along the
beach, his monologue is that of a poet and philosopher. Imagination, intellect, and memory combine with the senses to create
brightness and innocence. Everything, in substance and method
alike, is flowing. Mr. Bloom's monologue, as represented in the
next chapter, is darker and more sensuous. From lively concern
with the external world it passes easily to daydream and back
again. The monologue of each has a tone by which the quality
of individual experience is discovered and each has a proper
rhythm. Free association, which rivals logic for command of
Stephen's thought, is freer in Mr. Bloom's thought, and freest in
Molly's as it flows from one confusion to another. If syntax is the
shape of thought and punctuation is a sign of it, Mrs. Bloom's
thought, devoid of punctuation and syntactically liberal, is almost
thoughtless. Compared with Stephen's clear well-banked stream
and Mr. Bloom's wider, muddier, but still well-banked stream,
her enormous flow is less stream than flood.

    The quality of the individual stream and its tone change with
the time of day. By the lunch hour Mr. Bloom's mind, succumbing
to the demands of his body, has become heavily rhythmical and

ruminative. Hunger, united with erotic desire, and at last the tranquillity of digestion, provide a fundamental rhythm that Joyce described as peristaltic. As if contained in a stomach or a bowel, the images and memories of the stream occur, and recur, and occur again, each time with less distinction of shape. As the images disintegrate, the language becomes foody and less articulate: "I munched hum un thu Unchster Bunk un Munchday." In this alimentary context, the eyes of Parnell's brother, fixed no doubt upon the uncrowned king, become "poached eyes on ghost." No author has rendered the effect of body upon mind more profoundly or more happily expressed their agreement. When Mr. Bloom thinks of "the stream of life" in this chapter, it is impossible to determine whether he has reference to consciousness, the generations of man, or the passage of food through the body.

For his attention to man's nature, critics, calling Joyce cloacal, have alluded to an anal fixation. It is true that Joyce notices digestion and excretion. But in *Ulysses* these harmless necessary facts, taking their place in his celebration of mankind, are no more important, and no less, than they are in daily life. Mr. Bloom in the outhouse or breaking wind in the street is not unnatural nor is Stephen as he makes water on the beach. Not many readers notice what Stephen is doing. His functions are less obvious than Bloom's because Stephen, the symbol of man's intellect, is relatively indifferent to the flesh. Since Bloom, occupying the middle of Joyce's trinity, is the symbol of flesh and spirit, both parts of his nature must be established. It cannot be denied that in *Chamber Music* and *Finnegans Wake* Joyce seems devoted to urination. Most men retain something infantile; and all men, the analysts assure us, are either anal or oral in character. But those of the anal type are better stylists. If Joyce, like Rabelais and Swift, is of the anal type, we must make the best of it—as Joyce did.

His virtuosity is not limited to streams of life. Other techniques, such as question and answer, abound. The first chapter, which provides a transition between *A Portrait of the Artist* and the rest of *Ulysses,* is comparatively traditional. But next to the stream of consciousness, Joyce's favorite method is parody.

in the glory of the brightness, having raiment as of the sun, fair as the moon and terrible that for awe they durst not look upon Him. And there came a voice out of heaven, calling: *Elijah! Elijah!* And he answered with a main cry: *Abba! Adonai!* And they beheld Him even Him, ben Bloom Elijah, amid clouds of angels ascend to the glory of the brightness at an angle of fortyfive degrees over Donohoe's in Little Green Street like a shot off a shovel.

For change of pace, control, and multiplicity of effect Mr. Bloom's ascension is remarkable even in the work of Joyce.

Parody and stream are suitable for conscious experience. For semi-conscious experience Joyce used other methods, each appropriate to its matter. The scene in the cabman's shelter, for example, calls for special treatment. It occurs near the end of a long day. Bloom and Stephen, having wandered, are tired. Sentences trail off to no end. Phrases are trite, participles dangle, and infinitives split. All is flabby, stale, and fagged out. "Interest . . . was starting to flag somewhat all round." This kind of thing is good for its purpose, but after almost fifty pages of it, the reader may think there can be too much of a good thing. A second reading or a third, however, should change this hasty opinion.

Although much longer, the preceding scene cannot seem too long; for its union of horror and grotesque humor, immediate and compelling, holds the most general reader. Followed by his protector, Stephen goes to Mrs. Cohen's brothel. Stephen is drunk and Bloom is weary. To convey their mental condition to the reader Joyce projected the contents of their minds upon an imaginary stage. Speech tags, stage directions, and all the machinery of a play attend the mental action. There was nothing new about such dramatic projection of states of mind. The expressionists had used the technique for many years in painting and in literature. Joyce probably found his hint in Strindberg's *Dream Play;* but Flaubert's *St. Anthony* or the *Walpurgisnacht* of *Faust* may have had equal claim upon him. Joyce himself referred to his brothel scene as the *Walpurgisnacht* of *Ulysses*. His problem was not the dramatization of dream but of waking dream and hallucination. In their excitement and fatigue Bloom and Stephen succumb to fantasy and only at the end does full consciousness reassert itself. During the partial abdication of their conscious minds, they encounter people who are not there. Ghosts of the past, Stephen's mother, for example, and Bloom's grandfather, arise to plague them, and inanimate objects, often changing shape or multiplying, take on a personal life. Mr. Bloom's trouser button shares the mental stage with Virag, his paternal ancestor, who changes to bird and moth as he accuses Bloom. All the experiences of the day play their parts in this brilliant phantasmagoria.

Fantasy lies in the province of Freud and Jung, and there is reason to conclude that when Joyce wrote *Ulysses* he was more or less familiar with the ideas of both these analysts. While he was in Zürich during the first World War, Mrs. Harold McCormick, his patron, was also a patron of the local psychoanalysts. When she urged Joyce to submit to Jung's analysis, he refused. But talk of Jung and Freud was common in the cafés. Eugene Jolas says Joyce met Jung in Zürich. And Frank Budgen says that he often spoke to Joyce at this time of Freud's theories about dream. But the best evidence that Joyce knew about psychoanalysis and used it in *Ulysses* is internal.

On the Freudian level the acceptance of Bloom marks the resolution of Stephen's Oedipus complex. His unconscious attachment to his mother, conflicting with his conscious rejection of her, causes the guilt that oppresses him throughout the first two chapters. The "agenbite of inwit," as he learnedly names his guilt, is due in part to his rejection of Church and country, but these, of course, are parental symbols. Joyce establishes the maternal setting so elaborately by allusion and symbol that there can be no doubt about his purpose. In the first chapter Stephen thinks of Yeats' poem about Fergus. No text could be more appropriate for the maternal context. The theme of "Who Goes with Fergus?" one of the great poems of modern times, is escape from adult responsibility by retreat to childhood and the womb. Joyce used this poem to indicate Stephen's condition. Incompletely of ivory. Alluding to Stephen's former mariolatry, Joyce is identifying the mother with Mary and the Church.

But Nelson's pillar in the newspaper-office episode is plainly Freudian. With bitterness and humor Stephen tells the story of two Dublin virgins, who, after buying plums, ascend the winding stair to the statue of the "onehandled adulterer." They fear the pillar will fall as they look out at Adam and Eve's, Lawrence O'Toole's and the other landmarks of the city. As they stare at the promised land, they eat the plums and spit the stones through the railings. This Freudian fantasy, every part of which demands a standard interpretation, takes its place in Joyce's central theme of fertility and infertility. Joyce is using Freud to say that Dublin is sterile. From this wasteland, Moses or Bloom, ambiguously "horned and terrible," will lead Stephen to a more promising land.

Bloom's daydream fantasies in the brothel owe their substance to Krafft-Ebing, Freud's predecessor in the study of perversion. That Bloom's fantasy is free from the censor's interference is orthodox; for a pervert's ego does not inhibit his perversion. But it is likely that the details of Bloom's fetishism are less literal than symbolic. His symptoms, indicating what Krafft-Ebing calls masochism, are used to help establish Bloom as habitual sufferer and as one who invites his suffering. His perversion may symbolize the perversity of man.

Insanity and neurosis also appear during the course of *Ulysses*. Mr. Breen, who spends the day worrying about a post card and imagining persecution, is a madman, and Mr. Farrell, who walks outside the lampposts, has a compulsion neurosis. In these case-histories there is less Freud perhaps than common observation of mankind. But Mr. Bloom's slips of the tongue seem as Freudian as the free association of Molly's monologue.

Thinking of thought while teaching school that morning, Stephen finds in his "mind's darkness a sloth of the underworld, reluctant, shy of brightness, shifting her dragon scaly folds." As he broods on the octave at the piano in the brothel that night, he thinks of the fundamental and the dominant. These musical extremes symbolize many things: the reconciliation of opposites, for example, and the artist's relationship with reality. But they also symbolize the unconscious and the conscious minds. Such allusions point to Joyce's complete study of the unconscious.

Finnegans Wake is a dream. What happens in that vast, genial book happens in the conscious mind of a sleeper. Beneath this mind, directing it, the unconscious is at work. The sleeper is tolerant. Sometimes his unconscious acts like Freud's and, following "Jungfraud's Messongebook," sometimes like Jung's. Such references to Freud and Jung fill his learned sleep. None of these references is solemn; for Joyce's night is as comic as his day. Only pathos and tenderness and the memory of ancient guilt are allowed to interrupt the fun, and such interruptions are uncommon. Joyce has come to terms with reality. However serious about it he may be, there is "lots of fun at Finnegan's wake."

Since Joyce is dealing with the unconscious, one is tempted to call *Finnegans Wake* surrealistic. His "furloined notepaper" reminds one not only of Poe's purloined letter and of the condition of mammals but also of the fur-lined teacup of the surrealists; and one of Joyce's ladies has a torso equipped with bureau drawers that slide in and out after the manner of Dali's. But these are pleasantries. Although Joyce and the surrealists deal with the same materials, they are in opposite camps. The surrealists pretend no conscious control of their unconscious materials. Joyce was always in full control. No artist was ever more thoroughly aware of what he was doing and of its meaning. Combining all conscious knowledge with what his unconscious supplied, Joyce made deliberate arrangements. *Finnegans Wake* is elaborate design.

The first difficulty we encounter in this difficult book is the language. It is so strange and intricate that Joyce expected or, at least, said he expected the "ideal reader suffering from an ideal insomnia" to spend his life deciphering it. There are readers of this kind; but the others, who may want to read another book as well or do something else with what time is left them, may enjoy the surface and, with some help, penetrate it a little. The language of *Finnegans Wake* is based partly upon Freud. To understand it we must consider his theory of dreams.

A dream has two levels, the manifest and the latent. The

manifest is what we are aware of while we sleep and, sometimes, after we awake. The latent is the meaning concealed by manifest wonders. This meaning is generally sexual; for Freud's unconscious contains materials frowned upon by society and carefully repressed by the social ego. Between the two levels stands the censor, whose job is to see that we remain ignorant of what we have repressed and of the libidinous forces of our nature. These forces are so powerful that they must come out, but when they come, they have been disguised in such a way that our sleep is ordinarily untroubled. This disguise or the manifest dream is the result of a condition and a process. In the first place, because dreaming is very primitive and childish, it is immune to logic. In the second, the censor completes confusion by his dream-work. Taking the materials of the unconscious as they pass, he makes nonsense of them by symbolism, displacement, and condensation. We have already noticed the symbols of dreams. Displacement is that shift of emphasis by which the important is made to seem inconsequential. Condensation is making one thing out of two or more.

Since the dreaming mind confuses words with things, this triumph of economy is often verbal. Freud quotes several "comical and bizarre word-formations" in his book of dreams, and some of his ambiguities find their elements in two or three languages. Take the phrase "loves and fiches." This example, which is not from Freud, occurred in the dream of a bitter man who spent his days trying to reconcile scholarship, poverty, and love. The basis of his dream-condensation is the miracle of the loaves and fishes, which may suggest a religious escape from his troubles or a better way to get his food. Loaves and fishes could also represent the female and the male. With these meanings the punning censor combined the dreamer's other concerns. The word *fiches* is far from simple. *Fiche* is the French word for a small piece of paper with notes on it. *Ficher* is to force a sharp point into something. *Se ficher* is to mock. This many-leveled bilingual pun expresses, while concealing, the dreamer's situation and his mood.

This combination of elements is witty or almost witty. Freud makes it plain in his book on wit that this accomplishment, despised by earnest people who do not have it, is at many points analogous to dream. Wit and dream alike work by condensation and displacement. Far from being intellectual, this daytime parallel to dream owes its felicity to the unconscious. It becomes possible to understand how Mrs. Bloom can be a wit. But, however intellectual, her creator was a greater wit than she. A man whose unconscious could create "poached eyes on ghost" and the other puns of *Ulysses* was ready for hints from Freud.

Since dream is many-leveled, Joyce invented a many-leveled language for *Finnegans Wake*. In actual dreams puns occur singly. The almost continuous punning of Joyce's dream is less realistic, therefore, than suitable to his subject and purpose. Adapted from the hint in Freud's "intrepidation of our dreams" and elaborated by Joyce's ingenuity, this double talk is rich, efficient, and amusing. Allusions, distorted quotations, symbols, and displacements of emphasis—all the machinery of Freud, incredibly enlarged and multiplied—provide an instrument to harmonize tones and senses, times and places, keys and rhythms. His "quashed quotatoes" and "messes of mottage" suit "every person, place and thing in the chaosmos" and their constant change. His language, he says, is not a "riot of blots and blurs . . . and juxtaposed jottings . . . it only looks as like it as damn it."

Puns in two languages were not enough for the theme or for a linguist as great as Joyce. He compounded words out of such languages as he knew, and it is said that he knew about eighteen. Like his techniques, his languages suit the theme. Puns in Hebrew and Arabic embellish his account of Genesis, for example, whereas puns in Danish and Dutch accompany the Nordic moments of his hero. It is less easy to explain digressions into pidgin English, Esperanto, and pig Latin.

To those who disapproved of his puns, Joyce said that the Church of Rome is founded upon a pun—that of Peter and the rock—and what is good enough for the Church is good enough for him. To those who found his punning trivial, he replied that it is more often quadrivial.

By sound and rhythm Joyce's wonderful language appeals to

the ear. *Finnegans Wake* must be read aloud, and, as those who have heard Joyce's recording of the Anna Livia passage will agree, preferably by Joyce himself or at least by a Dubliner. But what he called his "counterpoint words" appeal simultaneously to the other senses as he implies in his distortion of the 113th Psalm, the one sung by Stephen emerging from the house of Bloom: *"Habes aures et num videbis? Habes oculos ac mannepalpabuat?"* You have ears and will not see? You have eyes but do not touch? The senses were never more thoroughly confused. For the confusions of most dreamers a surrealist movie would be adequate, but words alone could do for the complexities of Joyce's mind and for its character.

During the visit to the Wellington Museum the guide says: "This is big Willingdone mormorial tallowscoop. Wounderworker obscides on the flanks of the jinnies. Sexcaliber hrosspower." This passage is to be taken according to Freud. The mormorial tallowscoop, the marble-memorial-telescope-obelisk in the Park, is phallic and deathly too. The wounderworker combines wound with Mr. Bloom's wonderworker for curing flatulency. Sexcaliber hrosspower combines several symbols, all of them sexual: Excalibur or sword, caliber or gun, horse mixed with ross (the German for nag), and six-cylinder or car. As for the jinnies, they are girls.

Joyce also applied Freud's method to non-sexual themes. The following passage from the end of the fifth chapter, for example, unites food and religion:

> Deeply religious by nature and position, and warmly attached to Thee, and smearbread and better and Him and newlaidills, it was rightly suspected that such ire could not have been visited by him Brotfressor Prenderguest even underwittingly, upon the ancestral pneuma of one whom, with rheuma, he venerated shamelessly at least once a week at Cockspur Common as his apple in his eye and her first boys' best friend.

Tea, bread, and butter, and ham and eggs are confused with original sin, God, Adam and Eve, and Jesus. The connection between these apparent discords is Brotfressor Prenderguest. Brotfressor is professor and German bread-eater or taker-of-the-host. Prenderguest is French taker-of-the-guest or innkeeper. The word guest, which implies gast or ghost, hence host, settles the confusion. Food and religion unite in the sacrament and in the person of H. C. Earwicker, the godlike innkeeper, who, as we shall see, reconciles all contradictions.

Joyce reconciled Freud with Lewis Carroll, that earlier authority on dreams and their language. References to Carroll are as common in *Finnegans Wake* as references to Freud:

> And there many have paused before that exposure of him by old Tom Quad, a flashback in which he sits sated, gowndabout, in clericalease habit, watching bland sol slithe dodgsomely into the nethermore, a globule of maugdleness about to corrugitate his mild dewed cheek and the tata of a tiny victorienne, Alys, pressed by his limper looser.

It is difficult to see how commentators have found this an allusion to Swift. Tom Quad is in Christ Church College at Oxford where Carroll or Dodgson sat in clerical ease, writing about Alice, that tiny Victorian. There are references to Humpty Dumpty and to "Jabberwocky," Carroll's dream-poem in dream language. In *Through the Looking-Glass* Humpty Dumpty, who became one of the principal symbols of *Finnegans Wake,* explains the language of dream. "Jabberwocky" begins:

> 'Twas brillig, and the slithy toves
> Did gyre and gimble in the wabe . . .

" 'Slithy,' " says Humpty Dumpty, "means 'lithe and slimy.' You see it's like a portmanteau—there are two meanings packed up into one word." And he proceeds to explicate the further ambiguities as if he were William Empson and Alice the reader of a little magazine.

In his excellent essay on *Alice in Wonderland,* Mr. Empson shows that the book is not only a dream but a very Freudian dream. Alice goes along a passage, falls down a well, and enters a room with a door too small to permit her escape into the garden.

This fantasy proves Alice a fitting subject for psychoanalysis. "We grisly old Sykos," says the analyst in *Finnegans Wake,* "have done our unsmiling bit on 'alices, when they were yung and easily freudened." Sykos-on-alices is psychoanalysis and the analysis of Alice. In "He addle liddle phifie Annie," Alice, identified with Anna Liffey, is entirely normal. Liddell is the family name of Alice.

"Jabberwocky" is written not only in dream language but in looking-glass language as well. Alice cannot read it until she holds it to a mirror. *Finnegans Wake* is filled with looking-glass language or, at least, with an adaptation of it. "Kool in the salg and ees" is look in the glass and see. When transposed, the Egyptian goddess Aruc-Ituc becomes Cuticura. In another passage, equally Egyptian, there is a reference to "the key of Efas-Taem." This turns out to be the meat-safe. King Kram of Llawnroc is only King Mark of Cornwall, Tristan's uncle. Alice rapidly adjusts herself to such conditions.

His language provided by Carroll, Freud, and his own verbal distortions in *Ulysses,* Joyce composed his dream. At the beginning and the end of *Finnegans Wake,* the ambiguities are less obscure than in the middle where sleep is more profound. "Who do you no tonigh, lazy and gentleman?" The puzzled sleeper is aware of external happenings—the tapping of a leaf upon the windowpane—and he is disturbed by his snores. Nothing is quite certain. "Things flow about so here," Alice complains, trying to fix an object with her rational gaze. Here too a person suddenly becomes his opposite; one place or object merges with another, and changes or disappears before it can be identified. This is what we are accustomed to in dreams. Yet *Finnegans Wake* is not a realistic dream. It is too long and elaborate, and although individual at many points, too general. The summary of all dreams ever dreamed, it reveals the sleeping mind of man.

On the surface this general dream displays a rich confusion from which the story of a family emerges. The latent levels, at once hidden and revealed by puns, hints, and distortions, are various, sometimes sexual, but more often historical or philosophical. None of these is to be taken literally. Joyce's end was neither the naturalistic presentation of a night's sleep nor the recommendation of a philosophy, but the use of a night's sleep to represent the nature and condition of man and to create a work of art. The manifest and latent levels together compose an enormous symbol. Itself alone and not another thing or form, this symbol does what no other form can do and it says what a statement cannot say. This symbolic form is the meaning of the dream, and since symbol and book are one, *Finnegans Wake* is the meaning of *Finnegans Wake*. That sounds as if there were nothing more to say. Happily, however, there is something to say about the elements of the symbol and their relationship to one another.

The dream may not be there for its own sake, but it is a dream nevertheless, and a dream demands a dreamer. His identity is a problem. The first idea that critics had was that the dreamer is H. C. Earwicker, who is the hero of the book. But there are difficulties in the way of this notion. If Earwicker is the dreamer, the book must be his stream of consciousness and we the occupants of his sleeping mind. In the sixteenth chapter, however, we see him waking from his sleep and talking to his wife. Of course he may be dreaming that he is awake, but this is unlikely. At the end of the book, moreover, we occupy the mind of Anna Liffey, his wife. Earlier, the dream takes the forms of a quiz-program and of a text with marginal annotations. That Earwicker's dream could take these forms seems no less unlikely.

It is likelier, as Joseph Campbell has suggested, that the voice we hear is that of the professor who, like Vergil conducting Dante through the underworld, acts as guide. This thorough, contentious man, lecturing and quarreling all that night, is intolerably academic. Yet manifest confusion and the machinery of dream prove him to be asleep.

It is still likelier that Joyce himself is the dreamer. He was a learned man who, when he wanted to, could sound like a professor. If Joyce is the dreamer, that would explain the references to himself which occur on almost every page, not only in connection with Shem, who is clearly Joyce, but also in connection with Earwicker, for instance, and with Hosty, who writes the ballad about Earwicker. The dreamer could be the collective uncon-

scious, personified and speaking with the voice of sleep. But the
voice has a Dublin accent, and if it is that of the collective unconscious, it seems to come from Joyce's mouth. Such co-opera-
tion would account for a dream that is personal and yet the dream
of every dreamer.

The collective unconscious is Jung's invention. Consisting
of the deep, archaic layers of the mind, it is the deposit from
man's experience and development. This repository contains
materials from the family, the tribe, the nation, and from all
primitive and animal ancestors. Whereas Freud's unconscious,
containing repressed materials, is relatively personal, Jung's
is common to all men. Its top layer is personal, but under
this are those primitive symbols or archetypes that appear in
myth, dream, and literature. These archetypes, says Jung, are similar to the "collective representations" that Lévy-Bruhl talks about
in his study of the primitive mind.

Lévy-Bruhl, whom Joyce mentions several times in *Finnegans Wake,* performs several functions in the dream. One of
them may be to affirm Joyce's acceptance of the collective unconscious and its archetypes. But if Joyce took this idea from
Jung and Lévy-Bruhl, he changed it for his purposes. In addition
to the family and primitive man, he gave the collective unconscious command of all modern learning as well. This extension of
command would account for the foreign languages in *Finnegans
Wake* and for knowledge far beyond the individual dreamer's
capacity—unless, of course, that dreamer is Joyce himself. As
for the archetypal patterns, those of the father, the woman, and
rebirth are more conspicuous here than in *Ulysses.* The central
themes of *Finnegans Wake* are archetypal.

Joyce's dreamer or Joyce is dreaming of a family pattern
which seems to account for everything. The family consists of a
father, a mother, twin sons, and a daughter. Mr. Humphrey
Chimpden Earwicker is a publican. He and his family live over
the pub in the town of Chapelizod, a suburb of Dublin, on the
river Liffey near Phoenix Park. By many references to Sheridan
Le Fanu's *House by the Church-yard,* a novel about Chapelizod
and the Park, Joyce helps establish the feeling of locality.

Like Bloom, whom he resembles, Earwicker is the father-image. Hence godlike and patriarchal, he is the founder of cities and their ruler. Although a husband and father may seem to rule, his actual relationship with his family is intricate and changing. The domestic situation of H. C. Earwicker is exemplary.

This great family man has a name as complex as his situation. On one level Earwicker means dweller in Eire and on another it means earwig. Earwicker is only a dweller in Ireland. Of Nordic rather than Celtic ancestry, he represents the invading outlander. His mythical arrival from the sea is not only a Freudian image of birth but the coming of the Dane. Among the Gaels of Chapelizod he is almost as much a stranger as Bloom in Dublin. An earwig is supposed to creep into the ear where it annoys by a kind of gossip. In this capacity Earwicker is the embodiment of a dream and the reader's earwig. As the giant Forficules in the first chapter, he belongs, like his insect, to the family of Forficulidae.

Earwicker as giant, mountain, and hump is a Freudian symbol, both phallic and anal. He is the peninsular hill of Howth, which marks the northern limit of Dublin bay, and he is the Bailey lighthouse at Howth. His wife, Anna, is the river Liffey, whose feminine flowing gives the book its basic rhythm. All the male characters of *Finnegans Wake* are in a sense projections of H.C.E. as all the female characters are aspects of Anna Livia Plurabelle or A.L.P. Their initials, therefore, fill the dream.

Jerry and Kevin or Shem and Shaun, the twin sons of H.C.E. and A.L.P., are all the twins of history: Jacob and Esau, Cain and Abel, Tom Sawyer and Huck Finn, and Lewis Carroll's Tweedledum and Tweedledee. Shem, representing the inner, is Jung's introvert, and Shaun, representing the outer, is the extrovert. Together they compose H.C.E., in whom their characteristics are united. Their sister, Isabel, is a younger version of A.L.P. as Milly is a younger version of Molly Bloom. The monologues of Isabel or everygirl bear a family resemblance to those of Mrs. Bloom and Gerty MacDowell. H.C.E.'s affections, neglecting Shem and turning away from A.L.P., are centered upon Isabel and Shaun. But hints of incest are carefully obscured by the censor. Isabel appears in the disguise of another woman, and

Shaun hides under a variety of names. Even if Joyce is the dreamer, the censorship still operates; for Joyce as family man identifies himself with H.C.E. and that family with his own. In one of the footnotes of the tenth chapter he asks, "Is love worse living?"

Love at home is a difficult thing but love in the Park is sin. Earwicker is tempted and, like Adam, he suffers a "collupsus of his back promises." The Park is Eden under the name of Phoenix, and by this name it promises redemption after fall. For this reason St. Augustine's comment on the Fall, "O felix culpa," distorted and applied to Earwicker, becomes "O foenix culprit." Our immediate concern, however, is not his rise but his fall. As Adam, he is compared with all the fallers of history and legend, with Humpty Dumpty, for example, and with Tim Finnegan, who, in the Irish-American ballad that gives this book its title, is a fallen hod-carrier. Earwicker is Balbus not only because balbus is the Latin word for stuttering and Earwicker is a stutterer but because "Balbus was building a wall," and presumably fell from it. This sentence from a Latin primer, inscribed on the wall at Clongowes and reinscribed in *A Portrait of the Artist,* remained in Joyce's memory awaiting a suitable occasion. As master-gardener, Earwicker is Adam, but as Bygmester Finnegan he is Ibsen's master-builder, who fell from his tower. Echoes of falling Babel and Wall Street, rumbling through the first chapter, attend our hero's collupsus.

The nature of his sin remains unclear. Disguised by censorship, it evades attention. The professor tries in vain to penetrate the obscurity, and the judges of the court, in which Earwicker comes to trial, are no more successful. The evidence of the witnesses is irrelevant, immaterial, and incompetent. In these early chapters of the book the dream-work makes one character reappear under different names or, merging one event with another, confuses both. Nowhere else in the book are dream-conditions more authentic in appearance; for Earwicker's sin, like Adam's, is so central that it must be displaced.

We learn, however, that the sin involves two girls and three soldiers, whose identities are constantly shifting. Sometimes the girls seem to be projections of Isabel and Anna, and the soldiers Earwicker himself or his sons. Innumerable hints make it certain that the girls are relieving themselves. Earwicker, observing them, is either a voyeur, as psychoanalysts know the peeper, or else an exhibitionist. The soldiers meanwhile are observing him. Maybe he makes improper advances to the soldiers or maybe the whole scandal, as the work of gossips, is without foundation. All this is so obscure that even an experienced reader is apt to go astray. One commentator, for example, thinks a certain passage describes a body washing about in the surf. To be sure there is "a thud of surf," but it is heard through "minxmingled hair." Attention to the Latin pun in its context identifies the theme as two girls making water in the bushes.

Shortly after sinning or seeming to sin, Earwicker encounters a Cad with a pipe in the Park. The nature of this important meeting, which is closely associated with the sin, is equally unclear. The Cad, who may be Earwicker, may have asked Earwicker the time of day or else one of the two, like that pair in *The House by the Church-yard,* may have assaulted the other. According to the first version of this ever-changing story, Earwicker replies to the question by an unnecessary defense of his innocence. This guilty reaction starts the gossip that plagues the archetypal sinner throughout the dream.

The sin is archetypal in the sense that it summarizes the ancient pattern of the middle-aged man with one or two girls. Joyce compares Earwicker and his girls with Swift, Stella, and Vanessa. Further comparisons associate Earwicker with Tristan and his two Iseults, Lewis Carroll and Alice, Finn MacCool and Grania, and Daddy Browning and Peaches.

The gossip that follows such relationships is a major theme of *Finnegans Wake.* As they wash Earwicker's dirty linen in public, the two washerwomen discuss his domestic affairs and the affair in the Park. The twelve men who parade through the dream as the jurors at his trial and the customers of his pub represent public opinion. But the four old men, the chief projections of Earwicker's guilt, constitute what Freud would call the super-ego. The judges at Earwicker's trial, these men are the four elements,

the Four Masters, who composed the annals of Ireland, the four
provinces of Ireland, and the authors of the four gospels. These
censors often appear as "mamalujo," a condensation of Matthew,
Mark, Luke, John, mamma, and luga, a colloquial Russian word
for pool or puddle. The four of them—and, as Joyce implies, glory
be there's no more of them—stand for pious mother Ireland or
the Poor Old Woman herself.

In the fifteenth chapter, these four men, less annalists now
than analysts, question Yawn, who is a stage in the decay of
Shaun, Earwicker's favorite son and his surrogate. That "slipping
beauty" is supine upon an ancient barrow. Surrounding the
patient, the four psychoanalysts try to find the truth about "Bill
of old Bailey," the father-image in the depths of Yawn's unconscious. Bill means sword, beak, peninsula, and law. Bailey is
a lighthouse, and Old Bailey is a courthouse. This Freudian
condensation of father, Howth, and guilt identifies their quest.
But as they probe, Yawn's resistance, operating like the censor,
hides the truth about "Dodgfather, Dodgson and Coo," that
union of the Trinity with Lewis Carroll. Penetrating layer after
layer of the unconscious, the four analysts arrive at last at the
mother-image or A.L.P., who, speaking through Yawn, dismisses
the whole scandal as a frameup. "The park," she says, "is gracer
than the hole." The impatient analysts proceed to deeper levels
of the collective unconscious where all is primitive. But their
"exagmination" comes to nothing, and they are replaced by more
efficient analysts, who go further into these "traumaturgid" matters. Discovered at last, the father himself speaks from the depths
of Yawn, but only to proclaim himself the founder of cities and
the respectable victim of gossip. If there was a girl, she was a
niece; and anyway, he prefers his wife. Imputations of bisexual-
ism and other enormities are absurd. Seen "through alluring
glass," the sin of old "Lewd's carol" remains as obscure and
probable as ever. The conviction grows that his sin must be every
sin of every man.

As the analysts fail to get to the bottom of anything as
simple as that, so do the interpreters of the letter in the dump.
This letter, dug up from among the orangepeels by a hen is very

important. Seemingly a trivial communication from Boston, it
tells of family matters; yet under these simplicities it hides the
central matters of life and its meaning. Although childish in
appearance, it is difficult to decipher; for sometimes it seems
written in Futhorc or the runic alphabet and sometimes in
"siamixed twoatalk." The dump or midden from which it comes
is at once the place where life began, the repository of the past,
and the collective unconscious. A record of its archetypes, the
letter is literature.

The letter is A.L.P.'s comment upon H.C.E. or everybody.
She did not write it out herself, but dictated it to "a too pained
whittlewit laden with the loot of learning." Shem or Joyce wrote
it, and Shaun the Post carried it abroad. When Shem composed
this "poor tract of the artless," he was "unctuous to polise nope-
bobbies." It becomes obvious that the letter, while literature in
general, is *Finnegans Wake* in particular. Suggesting all the
themes of the book, the letter is the microcosm of a microcosm.

In chapter five the professor interprets the letter. Approach-
ing it with all the apparatus of scholarship, he examines the text
according to the methods of archaeology and then according to
the methods of psychoanalysis. As a sociologist with Marxist
leanings he traces party lines. As paleographer, he studies each
letter and mark of the "Tiberiast duplex." (Tiberian is a system
of punctuation used in the Old Testament.) But for all his tools
the professor can make nothing of the letter. His failure may
mean that scholarship and criticism, unable to deal with life and
art, must content themselves with externals.

Plain sense, humanity, and art also escape Shaun, the letter-
carrier, who, enraged by his inability to understand what he
carries, makes his girls cry "Shun the Punman." Owing his name
to Shaun the Post, the patriotic letter-carrier of Boucicault's play
Arrah-na-pogue, Joyce's Shaun represents the forces of convention. He points Lévy-Bruhl's Australian "deathbone," and the
quick are dead. Shaun's primitive, bourgeois magic, however, has
no effect upon the artist. Shem lifts the lifewand, and the dumb
speak. Emerging out of tree and stone, the washerwomen begin
their river-gossip. The lifewand that causes this miracle is the

ashplant Stephen carries about and with which he smashes the chandelier. Symbolizing the artist's creative power, this equally magic wand, at once phallic and vegetable, is identified in the fifteenth chapter of *Finnegans Wake* with Yggdrasill, the everlasting ashtree, and with the "beingstalk" or the tree of life. "Nobirdy aviar soar anywing to eagle it."

The power behind this bird-infested rod is Anna Livia Plurabelle. Far less individual than general Mrs. Bloom, A.L.P. represents the same creative energy. She animates every woman: Kate, Isabel, the washerwomen, and the original hen. The life force, evolution, and the poet's muse, she is less a character than a rhythm, less a person than a principle. The river or the water of life is her symbol. She flows through and is the "microchasm." Sometimes half-personified as a young goatish stream, "she ninnygoes nannygoes nancing by." Sometimes she is a cloud, and sometimes she assumes the body of Anna Earwicker. The wonder is that Joyce could give so much vitality and character to something so fundamental. Although we cannot describe her, we know when she is there. She exists in our minds by rhythm and tone, feeling and sound.

As she is identified with Mrs. Bloom, so H. C. Earwicker, identified with Mr. Bloom, shares many of that great man's characteristics, even his devotion to drawers. But H.C.E. is less individual than Mr. Bloom. Bloom is every man in our time. H.C.E. is every man in history. His initials produce Here Comes Everybody and "human, erring, condonable." Mr. Earwicker appears in the famous letter as Van Houten. This is not only an allusion to Jarl van Hoother, the Earl of Howth, but the name of a brand of cocoa. Mr. Bloom serves life's cocoa. Mr. Earwicker is also that sacrament, and "you and I are in him."

His Anglo-Saxon name contains the word "wick" or town. According to Skeat's *Etymological Dictionary,* to which Joyce was devoted, wick comes from Latin vicus, which means street or vicinity. This brings us by "a commodius vicus of recirculation" to Vico and the family cycle.

CHAPTER THREE

FAMILY CYCLE

IN the world, says preaching Shaun, nothing is certain, but in heaven you are "dead certain" to be nothing whatever forever. Having lost hope of heaven, Joyce had to replace one uncertainty by another. Man would do tolerably well for God; but to replace Christianity Joyce needed a system in which man could occupy the center. To please a mind at once scholastic and humane the new system should be intricate and inoffensive to reason. Joyce found what he wanted in history. The pattern of events in time gave him the sense of order and of belonging to a whole which, although in time, suggests eternity. Cyclical recurrence became his substitute for metaphysics. In *Ulysses* Stephen calls history a nightmare. *Finnegans Wake,* Joyce's "cyclological" novel, is the nightmare of history.

In this nightmare "the same roturns." We ride around Dublin in a jaunting car or follow the horses around their track or watch the girls dancing in a ring until all seems to move in circles. "Gricks may rise and Troysirs fall," for clothing and nations alike follow the pattern. The last sentence of the book comes round to meet the first, and *Wake* implies the cycles of sleeping and waking, day and night, death and resurrection. History and dream, says Joyce in the final chapter, are "a sot of a swigswag, systomy dystomy, which everabody you ever anywhere at all doze. Why? Such me."

His answer to his question is ambiguous. "Such me" may mean uncertainty, but it also means the certainty of participation

and the certainty of belonging to a large pattern, however meaningless and tiresome it may be. "Such me" is neither cynical nor
pessimistic, neither hopeful nor desperate. Its tone carries the
cheerfulness of acceptance and a kind of peace. Mr. Bloom's final
equanimity, which reflects that of his creator, follows his knowledge that he is part of a great cycle, the series of Molly's lovers.
He knows that "he is neither first nor last nor only nor alone in a
series originating in and repeated to infinity." With Ben Dollard
and Pisser Burke and Blazes Boylan he belongs to something
larger than himself. That cycle is natural, he concludes, and,
however injurious to vanity, inevitable.

Mr. and Mrs. Bloom occupy the family cycle that Joyce
presents more elaborately in *Finnegans Wake*. The Earwicker
family consists, as we have seen, of a father, a mother, two sons,
and a daughter, who, by interaction, produce not one but several
cycles. The coupling and uncoupling of father and mother compose the "bisexycle" that rolls along to the tune of a bicycle built
for two. After the marital bicycle come two tricycles: father,
mother, and children; and father, son, and father again. The latter, the important cycle of the book, is what determines its course.
Supplanting the father, the son becomes the father and is sup-
planted by the son. But the basic tricycle of father-son-father is
complicated by an epicycle and by the rhythmic alternation of
opposites. The epicycle is the father's temptation by another
woman, his daughter or her surrogate. The alternation of opposites is the rivalry between father and son or between son and son.
This organic machinery is what makes the world go round. History repeats the family cycle; for "everythings that is be will was
theirs."

Also the circular stream of life, the family is the "one sub-
strance of a streamsbecoming." The river of lives is nothing more
than "the regenerations of the incarnations of the emanations
. . . of Funn and Nin in Cleethabala," or of Earwicker and
Anna in Dublin. Their family is the pattern of all history and its
source. During their analysis of Yawn, the four old men doubt
his "cock and biddy story" of this pattern. But it becomes clear
that as his parents "met and mated and bedded and buckled and

got and gave and reared and raised . . . and bequeathed us their ills," they produced our history. "Ancients link with presents as the human chain extends, have done, do and will again." The embedded initials of A.L.P. and H.C.E. make this outline of history familiar. We recurrently meet our general parents in "cycloannalism, from space to space, time after time," because they underlie all things.

In the ninth chapter of *Finnegans Wake,* Glugg, an incarnation of Shem or Joyce, writes *Ulysses* and after writing it, proposes the exposure of his family. This will be *Finnegans Wake.* Always fascinated with parents, grandparents, and the other members of his family, he sees them as "the archimade levirs of his ekonome world." Literally interpreted, economy is managing the home, and liberally extended, it is the story of the world and Archimedes' lever for moving it. In the tenth chapter, Dolph, another incarnation of Shem, projects his family as a problem in geometry. Upon two central triangles he constructs two intersecting circles. Both triangles are A.L.P. because an Oedipal fixation, excluding the father, makes Shem usurp his father's place. With H.C.E. understood, the female creative triangle produces the circles of children, temptation, and history. These elementary figures and the "elipsities of their gyribouts" are "returnally reprodictive of themselves."

The family cycle is but one of many cycles that have fascinated men since Plato's time. In his "Timaeus" Plato sees history determined by the course of the great year, which like the cycle of day and night, summer and winter, and the precession of the equinoxes, brings everything around again. This vast cycle reappears in Vergil's fourth eclogue. Combining the three ages of classical myth with the Platonic year, the poet sees the golden age returning with another Argo and another Troy. In a chorus from *Hellas,* Shelley follows Vergil:

> A loftier Argo cleaves the main,
>   Fraught with a later prize;
> Another Orpheus sings again,
>   And loves and weeps and dies;

> A new Ulysses leaves once more
> Calypso for his native shore.

This anticipation of *Ulysses* leaves Shelley, one of Joyce's favorite poets, without equanimity. Although Shelley accepts Platonic determinism, he dislikes it, and, lamenting the return of so much hate and death, wishes that man could be freed from the temporal cycle. But Yeats, another of Joyce's favorites, accepts Shelley's cycle with something of Joyce's equanimity. In "Two Songs from a Play" Yeats adapts Shelley, Vergil, and Plato. Another Argo and another Troy give him the assurance that, as he announced in *A Vision,* his formidable essay on cycles, the great wheel maintains its destined course, shifting from gyre to gyre every two thousand years. Byzantium, his Utopia, where he can sing of past, present, and future, occupies a fortunate position in our cycle, at once in time and out of it. This place and his wheel appear in the tenth chapter of *Finnegans Wake:* "One recalls Byzantium. The mystery repeats itself . . . Gyre O, gyre O, gyrotundo!" Joyce thought it a pity that Yeats had not made the complexities of *A Vision* into a work of art.

Jung places the circle and the cycle of birth, death, and rebirth among his archetypes. From man's unconscious, where they abide, these patterns create his poetry and perhaps his history. Not only poets and psychologists but philosophers of history project cycles. In *The Decline of the West* Spengler, with whom Joyce was also familiar, argues from a metaphor. History, he says, is an organism that passes like a human body through three ages of youth, maturity, and decay. Once the natural cycle is over, a new one begins. In *A Study of History* Arnold Toynbee disagrees with Spengler. But, although not organic, Toynbee's history is more or less cyclical. Finding one pattern behind all civilizations, Toynbee treats them as contemporaneous parallels. Their common rhythm of growth and decay, however, is no more mechanical or deterministic than it is organic. It is a spiritual process and a matter of moral responsibility. Withdrawal and return according to the challenge of adversity may produce a cycle, but man is not bound to his wheel. While minor movements are recurrent, the major movement is progressive. Man can turn the wheel, says Toynbee, in whatever direction he desires. The survival of the fittest, the idea of progress, and free enterprise have never received more elaborate support.

Toynbee gave extraordinary expression to an idea that belongs more to the previous century than to our own. In the nineteenth century, ideas of progress commonly took the shape, not of a circle, but of a straight line, sloping upward. By no means an invention of that century or of the middle class, the idea of progress commenced during the renaissance when humanists, abandoning original sin, came to believe that man is good and infinitely perfectible. By the end of the nineteenth century this notion had been confirmed by astonishing advances in science. More science, more usefully applied, promised better houses, better food, and better men. But with the disappointment of this faith in man and his destiny, the straight line curved downward until, meeting itself, it expressed the vision of our century. Straight lines are out of fashion, and even Toynbee, expressing a demoded hope, makes use of circles, the comfort and expression of declining periods.

Yeats was cheerful because good times must follow bad. Cycles not only explain our present condition but give hope of another turn. Other cyclists get pleasure from form alone or else from feeling placed in a design. Although Joyce came at a time when others were thinking in circles, his design is peculiar in some ways, however typical in others. Like Toynbee's, it is neither entirely mechanical nor entirely organic, but centered in people. As if a humanist, Joyce placed man at the center; but he rejected progress and retained original sin. His vision is one of imperfect men falling and rising to no end. It was good, he felt, to contemplate a formal pattern and to be where he was not alone.

In *A Portrait of the Artist* Stephen broods about the cycle. Quoting Shelley's poem on the pale, weary moon, he is chilled by "its alternation of sad human ineffectualness with vast inhuman cycles of activity." A little later, thoughts of Shelley's lines, merging with an algebraic equation, carry him to the cycle of the stars, and he is filled with "cold lucid indifference." The sense of vast cyclic movement also accompanies his aesthetic experience on the beach. In his diary he observes that "the past is consumed in the present and the present is living only because it brings forth the future." These anticipations of *Finnegans Wake* are confirmed by Stephen's desire in *Stephen Hero* to bring the chaos of history into order by a diagram.

The general structure of *Ulysses* is cyclical. Mr. Bloom leaves his home and returns to it. Meanwhile, incidental references form epicycles upon the main design or help to indicate its shape. Stephen is always quoting "As it was in the beginning is now and ever shall be," but Mr. Bloom takes a livelier interest in these matters. The dance of the hours personifies for him the cycle of day and night. The process of eating, digesting, and excreting is another circle. Squads of policemen march out and back, the trams and racing cyclists make their rounds as, musing on life and death, he concludes that "both ends meet." One dies, another is born, a cityful passes, another takes its place—"cycles of cycles of generations." Such thoughts occur to him in cemetery and maternity hospital. After Gerty MacDowell limps away, his thoughts of sameness find expression in the phrase "History repeats itself." His thoughts of going and return evoke the image of Rip Van Winkle. These cyclical patterns suggest the philosophy of Giambattista Vico.

In *La Scienza Nuova* (1725) that philosopher expounds his philosophy of history. A Platonist yet a Baconian, an enemy of Descartes, Aristotle, and Aquinas, Vico was a pious Catholic. Since he was unable to advertise himself, he remained unknown in his lifetime and long afterwards.

The new science, says Vico, is the historical demonstration of Providence. With the aid of myth, language, and history, he traces the circle of an ideal history in which the real history of all nations turns. By finding the general laws that underlie particular events, he finds eternity in time. God, he says, is unknowable, and nature is unknowable too; for we know only what we have created. God alone can know nature; but we can know history. The laws of history are eternal, whereas we live in time. But these laws and patterns, implanted in our minds by divine Providence, are projected by man. Its agents, we create past, present, and future.

In each cycle of history there are three ages: the divine, the heroic, and the human, or the primitive, the semi-historic, and the historic. These three ages produce three sacred customs: religion, marriage, and burial, the first a product of the divine age, the second of the heroic, and the third of the human. After circular flux comes reflux. When one cycle is over, another begins, and, as the Phoenix rises from its ashes, history repeats itself. The first divine age that we know about is the period before the Trojan War. With that war the heroic age began. The human age of Athens and Rome led to the reflux, and from Rome's decay came a new age, as divine, barbarous, and cruel as the first. The feudal period of Europe brought a return of the heroic age. Vico lived in the human age, and it is easy to guess where we are.

After Noah's Flood, Shem founded the Semites, who are outside the cycle, while the children of Ham and Japhet, retiring to the forests, became mute barbarous giants. Then came the thunder. At this awful sound the giants found tongue, invented gods, and established families in convenient caves. The fathers, becoming patriarchs, ruled their sons and servants with divine severity. In the heroic age the family became the city, and the patriarchs aristocrats. Those who had found refuge in cities became plebeians. Their quarrel with their rulers brought democracy and with it the human age. At this point in every cycle, free enterprise or self-interest brings anarchy, which in turn invites dictatorship, monarchy or invasion and, eventually, a return to the golden age.

The three ages have languages suitable to each. In mute divine periods men use hieroglyphs: picture-writing, coats of arms, and fables. A heroic age brings proverbs and metaphor, the language of the imagination. In the human age, language becomes abstract or vulgar.

Attracted by Vico's interest in myth, language, and family, Joyce preferred him to other cyclists. Of them all, moreover, Vico seemed best adapted to Dublin; for that city has not only two circular roads and a Phoenix Park but a Vico Road as well. Joyce

was not a philosopher but an artist using philosophy as one element of an aesthetic whole. Vico's pattern appears in *Finnegans
Wake* not as an approved philosophy but as a structural device
and a parallel. Analogous to family development, Vico's cycles
help make domestic particulars general. Earwicker's family is not
there to illustrate Vico. He is there to give another dimension to
Earwicker's family. Joyce used Vico for *Finnegans Wake* as he
used Homer for *Ulysses*. They are but parallels and devices, and
it is wrong, as some have done, to give them too much weight.

References to "the Vico road" or to "Vi-Cocoa," which con-
nects Vico with Bloom and Earwicker, establish the parallel. Mr.
John Baptister Vickar, the producer of the spectacle on Joyce's
revolving stage, arranged our "millwheeling vicociclometer,"
which moves by the process of "eggburst, eggblend, eggburial and
hatch-as-hatch can." Such references to religion, marriage, burial,
and reflux, together with references to Michelet and Croce, authorities on Vico, let the learned reader know how universal Earwicker's family is. "It recurs in three times the same differently."

Vico's pattern is structural. *Finnegans Wake* is divided into
four books, the first three long and the last one short. The first
book has eight chapters, the second and third books have four
chapters apiece, and the fourth has one chapter. The first book is
Vico's divine age, the second his heroic age, and the third his
human age. The fourth book is the reflux that leads to the divine
again. In the first book we occupy a gigantic and fabulous world,
but since subsequent history grows out of this world, the elements
of the later ages are present in it. Each book contains the elements of the others, and each book contains the whole pattern.
Each chapter of each book is one of Vico's ages. In Book I the
first four chapters represent a complete cycle with its reflux. The
second four chapters repeat the cycle on another level. The four
chapters of Book II and the four chapters of Book III constitute
two more cycles. Joyce indicated the end of a cycle by the word
Silence. This word occurs in the third chapters of Book II and
Book III before the reflux. The main structure, therefore, is one
large cycle, containing four smaller cycles.

As each part contains the whole, almost every page contains

the whole. By innumerable sequences of religion, marriage, and burial Joyce turns smaller and smaller wheels within the principal wheels. Such sequences may take the form of religious, marital or sepulchral themes or they may take the form of brief allusions as in this account of Earwicker's career: he "speared the rod and spoiled the lightning; married with cakes and repunked with pleasure; till he was buried howhappy was he and he made the welkins ring with *Up Micawber!*" Mr. Micawber, who was expecting something to turn up, represents the reflux uncommonly well.

The hundred-lettered word that represents Vico's thunder appears at the beginning of the main cycle and here and there throughout the book. It generally means the fall of man or the father's anger. When that "phonemanon" occurs in the ninth chapter, at the beginning of the third cycle, the "unhappitents of the earth . . . terrerumbled" and, like Vico's primitives, cry "Loud, hear us!" In *Finnegans Wake* as in *The New Science*, the civilized world is the house "that Jove bolt."

Vico supplied social and political meanings for Joyce's family. H. C. Earwicker is by turns the giant, the patriarch, and the founder of cities. In the last capacity he comes into conflict with plebeians—the twelve customers of his pub. Fights with plebeians and the founding of cities occur, as they should, in the third chapters, or the human ages, of the third and fourth cycles, where the democracy to be expected in these periods is described as the "impovernment of the booble by the bauble for the bubble." That Vico's politics is not central but only a meaning added to the central family is plain in the following account of Earwicker. "Our awful dad," as he is called, "went puffing from king's brugh to new customs, doffing the gibbous off him to every breach of all size." This is very obscure. On the manifest level, Earwicker, walking down the street, doffs his collapsible opera hat to every large woman. At the same time he is a Guinness barge coming down the Liffey from the brewery to the new Customs House, lowering its smokestack for every bridge. On still another level, his passage follows the course of Vico's history from the burial of the king to the new cycle.

Joyce agreed that "the sibspeeches of all mankind have foliated . . . from the root of some funner's stotter." This means not only thunder, but the Fall, and Earwicker's stutter to the Cad in the Park. All three of Vico's languages appear in *Finnegans Wake*. The hieroglyphic is best represented by the fables, the rebuses, and Earwicker's coat of arms. Metaphor, proverbs, and vulgar speech abound. In contexts of burial or democracy and at the end of cycles the language is legal and abstract as in the report on the family in the sixteenth chapter. The letter, of course, reveals three kinds of language.

Evolving from the patriarchal family, Vico's cycles fit Joyce's pattern. The Earwicker family supplies a structure to which the Viconian structure corresponds. Book I concerns the father, the mother, and Shem, the mother's favorite son and her spokesman. The first four chapters are the cycle of the father from birth to death and rebirth. The second four chapters are the cycle of the mother from her original letter to her renewal as the river. The eight chapters of Book II and Book III concern the father, the mother, and Shaun, the father's favorite son and his successor. In Book IV, the mother, again a river, again renews herself and her family.

The first chapter of Book I establishes a pattern that is equivalent to one of Jung's archetypes in the collective unconscious or to the formula impressed upon the mind by Vico's Providence. The family and all of man's history evolve from this pattern. The hero of the chapter is not a person but the pattern, which, variously manifested throughout history, underlies it and gives it shape. In the opening pages, the shaper assumes the character of Tim Finnegan, the hod-carrier of the Irish-American ballad, who falls, dies, and wakes at his wake. So personified, he reveals the fundamental pattern of death and resurrection from "Finn no more" in chapter one to "Finn again" in chapter seventeen. The mourners at his wake cry: "Mister Finn, you're going to be Mister Finnagain!" History is his wake and we are his mourners. Finn will never return as a person because he has never been one, but he revives, dies, and revives again at all times in every person. He is in Adam and Jesus and Jakes McCarthy. In the beginning the scenery is that of the early chapters of Genesis before the Flood and long before the thunder that started the cycles of history. As its fundamental pattern, Finn precedes cyclical history, and as it proceeds, he is its "sameold . . . adomic structure."

Earwicker, the father, is the embodiment of Finn. Repeating the pattern of fall and wake, ever going, ever coming, he reappears in every age, now divine, now heroic, now human. He "moves in vicous cicles yet remews the same." The catalogue of his names extends over many pages. He appears in countless forms because he is all men as Finn is their pattern. Adam, Noah, a primitive giant, Napoleon, and Parnell by turns, he is "more mob than man." In the modern times of the fifteenth chapter he becomes "Mr. Tupling Toun of Morning de Heights with his . . . rambling undergroands." This reference to Morningside Heights and the subway makes it seem likely that he is at Columbia University. References a few pages later to Riverside Drive, Spuyten Duyvil, Greenwich Village, and the Bowery confirm his whereabouts. But as he ends the cycle at that place, his son, repeating him, will also be Finn again—and maybe his daughter will go to Barnard.

Earwicker is the "handpicked" husband. Anna Livia Plurabelle, who is sometimes a hen, "picking here, pecking there," is the picker. Older and wiser than he, she belongs to the original design, and her "natural selections" help to turn the wheel. After the fall of Finn, she picks up his pieces, puts them into her "nabsack," and hands them to his children. After Earwicker's fall in the same park, she hands gifts from her mailbag. She comforts the fallen father and, renewing him through his children, lifts him up again. As Kate, she presides over the museum in the Park, where Finn is lying, and she presides over magazine and dump. The magazine is the arsenal in Phoenix Park to which Swift devoted an epigram. The dump is sometimes a midden or a barrow. Nabsack, museum, magazine, and dump, all containers of Finn's remains, represent tomb and womb, the end and origin of life. She is the custodian of life and its transmitter. According to a passage in Latin in the tenth chapter, the Liffey or the river of life rises in the dump and flows from it to the sea—from the remains of the father to the father himself.

The course of her "movely water" is circular. After she reaches the sea, she rises from it as a cloud and falls as rain. At the end of the fable of the Mookse and the Gripes in the sixth chapter, she is a cloud:

> She cancelled all her engauzements. She climbed over the bannistars; she gave a childy cloudy cry . . . And into the river that had been a stream (. . . her muddied name was Missisliffi) there fell a tear, a singult tear, the loveliest of all tears . . . for it was a leaptear. But the river tripped on her by and by, lapping as though her heart was brook.

Nuvoletta, the cloud, is A.L.P. when young or her daughter Isabel. That young lady and her twenty-eight schoolmates, who are always dancing in a round, represent a moon or the cycle of a month, in particular the February of leap year. That is why Nuvoletta is a leaptear when she rains. Moon and month are feminine, and leap year means the pursuit of man.

Women not only pick the father and pick him up when he is down but they cause his fall. They are the temptresses in the park or their own rivals for his favor. A.L.P. is Isabel and Isabel is her father's temptress. Managing his fall and rise, women make him feel important. Some men know this, but Isabel knows it without going to school, for it is "the law of the jungerl." The invocation to Anna at the beginning of the fifth chapter may seem offensive because it parodies the words and rhythm of the Lord's Prayer. But she demands the most solemn language. As "Bringer of Plurabilities," she enables the father to manifest himself.

God the Father in *Ulysses* is a metaphor for Bloom. Although God's place in *Finnegans Wake* is more puzzling, it is probable that God is a metaphor for Finn, Earwicker, Shem, and Shaun. If God is there apart from these godlike manifestations, He is unknowable. Sometimes, as in references to the Maker, Joyce seems to imply a God apart from manifest reality, but, when examined, these references apply to Finn or H.C.E. or else they are ambiguous. Take, for example, "the Great Sommboddy within the Omniboss." Sommboddy applies equally well to God, Finn, or the sleeper, and Omniboss applies to God, Finn, H.C.E., or the universe. If science can tell us nothing about that Sommboddy, says Joyce, perhaps art can tell us something about his manifestations.

Divine thunder in *Finnegans Wake,* like the thunder in *Ulysses,* is only thunder. It may signify man's anger or his guilt, but, like Vico's thunder, which invites a fictive Jove, it is a natural phenomenon.

While Vico's Providence, residing in the mind of man and acting through it, is ostensibly divine, it is implicitly human. Piety kept Vico from seeing the humanity of his design. Skepticism and the aid of Jung, perhaps, enabling Joyce to pursue Vico's implications to their logical end, transformed divine Providence into archetypal pattern or racial memory. By retaining the language and machinery of the divine, however, Joyce gave divine weight to human pattern. In this metaphor, which united his religious and his human interests, he found suitable expression.

As the immanent pattern, Finnegan is godlike. At his wake he becomes the sacrament, and his mourners feed upon his body. "Grampupus is fallen down but grinny sprids the boord." Grinny, the woman who picks up his fragments and sets the table, is not only grandma but Grania because Finnegan is Finn MacCool, the Irish hero. As a fish, Finnegan is also Finn MacCool's salmon of wisdom. Becoming parr, smolt, and grilse, three stages in the life-cycle of the salmon, the edible giant suggests the Viconian round. But the fish is a traditional symbol of Jesus Christ. While the disciples eat him for supper, Finn seems "brontoichthyan." A thunder-fish unites Jove and Jesus.

The death and resurrection of Finn and of Earwicker, his historical embodiment, suggest Frazer's *Golden Bough.* The volumes on Attis, Osiris, and Adonis, in which Frazer follows the pattern of the dying, reborn, and sacramentally eaten god, must have been as useful to Joyce as they were to Eliot when he wrote *The Waste Land.* Frazer's vegetable gods, reproducing the cycle of the seasons, ensure fertility. They die with the flowers in winter and recover in the spring. Earwicker, who is compared with the flowers of spring, is surrounded with Frazer's holy vegetation—ivy, holly, and mistletoe. Like Frazer's gods, he is castrated, hanged or torn apart. "They have waved his green boughs o'er him as they have torn him limb from lamb"; for Bacchus, Orpheus, and Jesus are his parallels. He is buried under a lake in order to restore fertility to the wheat. As the host in his pub, he is eaten by his customers. He is the "mangoat." Man-god and scapegoat, he atones for the sins of men. But always he revives again, for he is not only a "Cooloosus," the re-embodiment of Finn MacCool, but he is "fincarnate."

Searching history and literature, Joyce found other parallels for Earwicker. He is John Peel and Dick Whittington, both of whom illustrate going and return, and he is Tennyson's King Arthur, who will return to the round table as the old order, changing, yields place to new. But a more important parallel is *The Book of the Dead*. This hieroglyphic document, found in Egyptian tombs, contains prayers, incantations, and advice for the use of the dead. With its aid, they can leave Amenta or the underworld and come forth by day. Journeying to Heliopolis, the city of the Phoenix, they can share the resurrection of Osiris and the cycle of Râ or the sun. Death and resurrection, the conflict of opposites, and the cycle of night and day commended this document to Joyce. The many references to it in *Finnegans Wake* take their place with allusions to Ibsen's *When We Dead Awaken* in the structure of analogies.

According to Freud, God is a projection of the father-image. As a father, Earwicker is god. His wife addresses him as the "Mosthighest," and even the four old men recognize him as "Gun, the farther." When Joyce's Saint Patrick prays to the "Great Balenoarch" or the whale-ruler, he seems to mean Hobbes' Leviathan or mankind or Earwicker. As Earwicker's son, Shaun inherits the divine pattern. He too goes through the cycle of death and resurrection and in his turn he is the sacrament. But living in the human age, he is far less holy about it than his father has been. In the fourteenth chapter, as both priest and victim, Shaun offers the sacrament to the twenty-nine girls. "Drink it up, ladies," he says, and takes it himself as if it were Bloom's cocoa: "That was a damn good cup of scald! You could trot a mouse on it."

Even Shem, the other son, is divine. In the tenth chapter, Shem, as Dolph, draws a diagram of circles. As we have seen, this represents his mother and, by implication, his father. In Genesis, God created the world with a circle, the Hebrew word for compasses. By analogy, Shem with his compasses has created a world. This circular disclosure of his parents' secrets is *Finnegans Wake*. As literary creator or "Shapesphere," Shem is god.

Creation is the descent from unity to multiplicity. Whether unity descends into a world, a book, or a child, the creative process is the same. The Cabala describes it as a series of emanations from God to the diversity of matter. This "Sephirotic Tree" of emanations seems to have impressed Joyce, who alludes to it at the beginning and at the end of the tenth chapter. As Ainsoph, the Cabalistic God, Earwicker is one, his wife is zero, and together they are ten, the number of completeness. "Maker mates with made," and the seven wonders of the world follow their union. As God descends the Sephirotic Tree, so Earwicker begets his children. The fall of man, another descent from unity to multiplicity, is also creative. "You wish to ave some homelette," the chef remarks. "Your hegg he must break himself." All history and the home evolve from the fragments of Humpty Dumpty, as from the fall of Adam come our sorrow and redemption. Earwicker's sin in the Park is like Adam's in Eden. "O felicitous culpability," cry his descendants, "sweet bad cess to you for an archetypt." These allusions to Genesis and the Cabala serve as parallels for fatherhood. The family man, like God or Adam, descends or falls into his children.

When Earwicker, descending from one to two, begets twin sons, he causes a quarrel of opposites that will continue until it is resolved in unity and a new father is ready to descend again. Earwicker's twins represent the two sides of his nature. A union of Shaun and Shem, he wears the face of Shaun over the innards of Shem; for Shaun is always dominant and Shem recessive. They are the good and evil or the Mick and Nick in him, and he is the "nikrokosmikon." The riddle of the Prankquean in the first chapter concerns the father and his twins: "Why do I am alook alike a poss of porterpease?" Following the Viconian pattern, that mysterious lady comes and goes three times to ask this question. Earwicker cannot answer it, but her meaning is plain. The keeper of a pub, he is porter, and his sons are as like as two peas. As their union, he is porterpease, and they, although identical, are opposites. That is "peacisely" why we have a "porterfeud," and that is why, when they are quarreling as "castor and porridge"—Castor and Pollux combined with Jacob and Esau—Baudelairian Shaun calls Shem "my shemblable! My freer!"

Their conflict is the process of history and its machinery: "No Sturm. No Drang." Representing all conflicting individuals of history and legend and all conflicting forces (such as heart and head, masculine and feminine, nation and individual), the twins also represent all wars and political quarrels. Their continual battle and periodic reconciliations occupy a large part of *Finnegans Wake*.

The simplest of these quarrels and one of the most attractive is that of the Ondt and the Gracehoper in the thirteenth chapter. This fable, based upon La Fontaine, concerns the artist and society. Shaun, who is the industrious ant (ondt is Danish for evil), represents the forces of convention and piety. Shem, who is the improvident grasshopper, is the rejected artist, wasting his time on useless things. Their quarrel is also one between extrovert and introvert. After he has discredited Shem, extroverted Shaun claims that if he wanted to, he too could write a book. He would "introvent" it.

The fable of the Mookse and the Gripes or the fox and the grapes in the sixth chapter is more complex, less personal, and gayer. Hanging from the limb of an elm, the Gripes disputes with the intruding Mookse. Their conflict, largely political, is that of Pope Adrian IV and Henry II with the Irish, a quarrel that is also the subject of the fable of the bull in *Ulysses*. In the debate of the Mookse and the Gripes, however, other political overtones are present: Elizabeth's projected marriage with Alençon, the dispute between Pope and anti-Pope, that between the Eastern and Roman churches, and those between the English and the Irish and "the Marx and their groups." As elm, the Gripes, who represents Shem, means life and growth; as stone, the Mookse means fixity and death. Together they represent the two banks of the river Liffey. Nuvoletta's attempt to reconcile these conflicting opposites is a failure. All she can say is what all women say of men: "There are menner."

But women are commonly among the most successful agents of reconciliation. In the dispute of Burrus with Caseous, which follows that of the Mookse with the Gripes, Margareena succeeds, where, as Nuvoletta, she has failed. Burrus and Caseous are not only Brutus and Cassius but butter and cheese, and their reconciling sister is margarine. Burrus and Caseous, angles B and C of an "isocelating biangle," are incomplete. By rejecting them and choosing Antonius, "a wop," Margareena completes the Roman triumvirate and, by adding angle A, completes the triangle. Triangle BCA is now equivalent to triangle HCE or the father. In the conflict of Justius with Mercius, the twins are reconciled by ALP, the maternal triangle. "Sonnies had a scrap," she says, and draws them to her.

Women are not the only agents. After Earwicker manifests himself in the tenth chapter, the twins begin their necessary fight. Because they are working at their geometry lesson, they are sometimes Rhombulus and Rhebus, but their family knows them as Dolph and Kev. Kev hits Dolph, but instead of returning the blow, Dolph forgives his brother. This reconciliation of opposites is the work of the artist. The introvert as artist can understand and forgive the extrovert, but the extrovert can neither understand nor forgive the introvert. By accepting the hostile world, the introvert reconciles himself with it, and the two become one in his art.

After Taff has struck Butt in the eleventh chapter and Butt has forgiven his brother, this vaudeville team takes communion. To demonstrate their unity they change places, becoming Tuff and Batt, and pledge "fiannaship." The Fianna is the band of Finn MacCool. Therefore the sons have become one in their father. This seems odd because Butt has just shot the Russian general and that officer is his father. But to be reconciled in the father it is necessary to destroy him; for opposites reconciled become the father. That paternal product of extremes reconciles Glugg and Chuff, whose battle over the twenty-nine girls rages throughout the ninth chapter. Isabel, who takes the part of temptress, incites this battle of orthodox against heterodox and of the popular against the individual.

The girls ask Glugg to guess their riddle. While he tries in vain to think of "heliotrope," the answer they require, they swarm around Chuff, who, as extrovert, gets what he wants without trying. Tittering "heliotrollops" now, they turn "towooerds him in heliolatry." Heliotrope, a theme recurring throughout the book, is not so difficult as Glugg thinks. It means turning to the sun. Since the twenty-nine girls represent the moon or else are represented by it, they naturally turn to the sun, and Chuff or Shaun is the son. "Heliotropolis" combines heliotrope with the city of the Phoenix. As the cycle renews itself, Shaun as son will take his father's place.

That is suggested in the last chapter when Shaun reappears as Kevin in Newer Aland. The name of this place is significant. Let New Zealand represent the end of the old cycle. Then, as the wheel revolves from Z to A, it must certainly come to Newer Aland. The hero of a saint's life, which takes the form of a maternal fantasy, Kevin retires to Yeats' Lake Isle of Innisfree with a portable bathtub-altar. Sitting in it, he meditates upon the renewal of man by water. "Yee," he cries as he feels the cold. Saint Kevin Hydrophilos of this hilarious and kindly legend is not yet a father, but, reconciled with Shem, he will be his father's successor. Appearing to be Shaun alone, he will carry the seeds of his opposite within him so that when he descends into creation he too may beget conflicting sons.

Being one and two at once is less mysterious than being one and three. Earwicker's internal division, projected and personified, appears in a series of conflicts that are similar to those of Shem and Shaun. But differences in tone and character distinguish the conflicts of the created sons from those of the potential sons within him. The internal quarrels are more dreamlike and somewhat less comprehensible.

All of Earwicker's conflicts are versions of his encounter with the Cad in the Park. This very general meeting of victim and antagonist, made more general by references to Genesis and ancient history, is confused by the alternations of the contenders. Each becomes the other. This confusion is linked by cross-references to the debate of Mutt and Jute in the first chapter. Here in the divine age, the contenders are very primitive and imperfectly articulate. Mutt gets his name not only from the comic-strip character but from Vico's mute giant. He and Jute are a stick and stone or a native and a Danish invader on the field of Clontarf. When reconciled, they will become the modern Irishman. In this as in Earwicker's other civil wars, there are references to the Mookse and the Gripes; for Shem and Shaun take up and carry on the old man's battles. All battles, including Waterloo and Balaklava, find their pattern in his head. As Buckley who was to shoot the Russian general and as that general, Earwicker repeats himself. If we wonder how a man so contrary can get along with himself, we must remember that nobody wins his internal wars. The confused antagonists fight to a draw; for each of them seems unaware which one he is or what he is fighting for. The coincidence of opposites, Earwicker maintains a balance among them. But his elements and their projections are so various that it is hard to "idendifine the individuone."

The coincidence of opposites belongs to many cyclical systems. In Yeats' great wheel, for example, the twenty-eight phases of the moon produce the clashing and uniting of antitheses: the subjective and the objective, the self and the anti-self. But Vico is silent about opposites. To supplement Vico by the discords and concords, all the quarrels and reconciliations, that the cyclical family demands Joyce turned to Nicholas of Cusa and Giordano Bruno.

Nicholas of Cusa, a fifteenth-century cardinal troubled by pig-headed nuns, was a politician and a mystic. The central tenet of this philosopher is the coincidence of contraries. They coincide in God, in whom all opposites are reconciled. He is the one and the many, the possible and the actual, the maximum and the minimum. Reality is double and correlative. One side is God; the other is creation. But the finite is implicit in the infinite and the infinite is explicit in the finite. Multiplicity demands unity. Unity involves the possibility of the many. Existence is a circle which begins and ends in God, turning from the infinite to the finite and back again or from unity to multiplicity and back to unity. God, says Nicholas, is unknowable.

This sounds as if he had Earwicker and the twins in mind. We can be sure, however, that Joyce had Nicholas in mind when he wrote *Finnegans Wake*. Professor Jones, in recounting the history of Burrus and Caseous, says that he is not endorsing "the learned ignorants of the Cusanus philosophism in which old Nicholas pegs it down that the smarter the spin of the top the sounder the span of the buttom." *De docta ignorantia* or learned ignorance is the principal work of Nicholas. The top, to which Professor Jones refers, is God, and the bottom is manifestation in time and space. In the third chapter Earwicker says: "Now let the centuple celves of my egourge as Micholas de Cusack calls them . . . by the coincidance of their contraries reamalgamerge in that indentity of undiscernibles where . . . this outandin brown candlestock melt Nolan's into peese!" Nicholas himself appears in this passage as the reconciliation of Mick and Nick. Earwicker's Freudian candlestick, begetting twins as like as peas and reconciled in peace, brings us by references to brown and Nolan to Bruno of Nola.

Giordano Bruno of Nola, a sixteenth-century philosopher, heretic, and martyr, also believed in the coincidence of contraries. But whereas Nicholas found the contraries of the world to be one in God, Bruno, identifying God with the world, found contraries united in the world. Although God is unknowable, he held, we can get some notion of Him through nature in which He is immanent. In nature, the divine container of opposites, each thing is the starting-point of its contrary. Therefore reality is circular, and decay, for example, is the beginning of generation. Each thing contains the whole. If in the minimum all opposites coincide, the minimum is the maximum. Love is hate and hate is love. For these tiresome confusions of one thing with another they burned him at the stake.

But Joyce found Bruno attractive. A relapsed Dominican, who retained an affection for ritual while rejecting dogma, could not but appeal to the relapsed, ritualistic Jesuit, who felt himself martyred by the world. Like Bruno, Joyce was the coincidence of Catholic and heretic. To discover Bruno while one is a student at a Jesuit school is irregular, but Joyce may have come across Pater's essay on Bruno in the *Fortnightly Review* and read his works for practice in Italian. When Father Artifoni, the Italian teacher in *Stephen Hero,* admonishes Stephen for reading Bruno's *Triumphant Beast,* Stephen replies that if Bruno was a terrible heretic, he was "terribly burned." *The Triumphant Beast,* in which Bruno attacks the Church's tyranny over mind and speech, expressed Joyce's own rebellion against authority, and a quotation from Bruno in *The Day of the Rabblement* (1901) supports Joyce's individualism. To Bruno, Aristotle was the symbol of authority. It is curious to find an enemy of Aristotle attractive to Joyce at a time when he was making his aesthetic theory out of Aristotle and Aquinas. But as the Jesuits observed, Joyce had separated aesthetics from belief. Later in life he was more in sympathy with Bruno than with Aristotle. In *Ulysses,* Stephen still calls for aid upon the scholastic philosophers, and in *Finnegans Wake* Shem is sometimes identified with Aquinas, but for every reference to Aquinas or Aristotle in *Finnegans Wake* there are fifty to Bruno.

It is probable that the donkey which follows the four conventional old men about is the ass by which Bruno symbolized unquestioning submission to authority. But more important than this is Joyce's mention in *Finnegans Wake* of *Eroici Furori,* Bruno's mystical acceptance of nature. Bruno was of value to Joyce not only in support of rebellion but for the idea of an immanent God, who is hardly to be distinguished from Vico's Providence or H. C. Earwicker. Bruno's idea that everything is implicit in anything and his idea of the cycle of opposites fitted the Viconian system and the family cycle. If Earwicker's family is the minimum, it is also the maximum. Dublin, which contains not only a Vico Road but a bookstore named Browne and Nolan, is as universal as Bruno of Nola. In the mathematics of *Finnegans*

Wake Earwicker and the twins can arrive at anything by "Browne and Nolan's divisional tables."

Bruno and Nola, variously distorted, appear at moments of discordant concord throughout the book, especially when equal opposites are "polarised for reunion by the symphysis of their antipathies." Tristopher and Hilary, the twins of the Prankquean legend, get their names of sadness and joy from Bruno's motto: *In tristitia hilaris hilaritate tristis.* At the beginning of the fable of the Mookse and the Gripes the professor scolds Bruno Nowlan, one of his pupils. At the end of the story the same pupil is Nolan Browne, his own opposite. Everywhere Bruno's contraries work in harmony with Vico's cycles. The sense of the Latin passage in the tenth chapter is something like this: according to the wisdom of Giordano and Giambattista, history flows like a river from a dump between rival banks.

This and the other accounts of the historical process bring Hegel to mind. Joyce mentions him once or twice and often uses the words dialectical, antithesis, and synthesis. Hegel's synthesis resembles Bruno's coincidence. But Hegel's antithesis follows his thesis in time, whereas Bruno's thesis and antithesis are simultaneous. Hegel serves to confirm Bruno and Nicholas, while Bruno and Nicholas correspond to the family pattern.

Since Earwicker alone is the coincidence of opposites, he alone is complete. His battling sons are incomplete until their moment of union. Each son is necessary to the other and his complement. In their battle, Joyce does not favor one side or the other. He may identify himself with Shem, but he knows that Shem needs Shaun as Shaun needs Shem.

Meanwhile the battle of inner and outer proceeds, Swift representing the inner and Sterne the outer. Together they unite the imagination and the bottom. The inner is also represented by George Berkeley, Irish philosopher and bishop of Cloyne. That subjective idealist, who doubted the existence of the material world, occupies the thought of Stephen in *Ulysses* as he walks the shifting beach: "The good bishop of Cloyne took the veil of the temple out of his shovel hat: veil of space with coloured emblems . . ." Stephen's thought, concerned with possibility and with actuality in time and space, finds Berkeley a convenient symbol. In *Finnegans Wake* Berkeley reappears as a customer in the pub and less directly in allusions to "tar water," that curious beverage to which the bishop devoted a monograph. But his principal appearance is in debate with St. Patrick in the last chapter. Like Mutt, Berkeley is the native; and, like Jute, Patrick is the foreign intruder. As the Archdruid, Berkeley defends metaphysics and imagination against Patrick's devotion to matter. Upholding the reality that is hidden behind the veil of the phenomenal world, Berkeley loses the debate to practical Patrick.

The idealistic druid wears a rainbow-colored mantle. Rejecting the "Irisman" and his rainbow, Patrick comes out for black and white, especially the latter. Their debate is one between the seven colors of the spectrum and their concord in white light. To understand this conflict we must consider the meaning of the rainbow. From the beginning of *Finnegans Wake* to the end, this celestial sign rivals thunder in importance as a symbol. Seven in one, the rainbow means unity from diversity, and by its shape it implies the cycle. It is a symbol of peace after conflict, of renewal, and of harmony. The music of the play in the ninth chapter is arranged by those eminent composers L'Archet and Laccorde. The twenty-eight girls, dancing in a round, are rainbow girls, whose colored cycles hold promise of renewal for mankind. When the druid favors the rainbow, he has all these meanings in mind but he intends another meaning as well. Having attained the seventh degree of wisdom, he can see the seven true colors of reality. To simple Patrick, from whom reality is veiled by illusion, these colors appear to be the white of common day. Only the seer, the philosopher, and the imaginative man can penetrate the veil of illusion to the multi-colored richness it conceals. But in Patrick's white light the colors, although invisible, are present. Art, the coincidence of Berkeley's vision with Patrick's, is the power to see the colors in white light.

It will be recalled that the twenty-eight rainbow girls and Isabel, the twenty-ninth, demand the answer to a riddle. If heliotrope, the proper answer, means turning to the sun, it must involve white light and its seven elements. Heliotrope, the gift of seeing reality, is seeing the true lights of the sun together with their common appearance. Glugg's failure to guess this riddle is easy to understand. Asking the most difficult thing in the world, the girls demand complete insight into reality or seeing the thing in itself through its manifestation. The girls have this power because women are born with knowledge of reality. But Glugg cannot have it until, uniting with Chuff, his worldly antithesis, he will see white light and the seven colors.

Meditating the subjective and the objective, the possible and the actual as he walks that beach, Stephen crushes shells beneath his feet. These shells or husks, like Mr. Deasy's money, are symbols of the outer. The inner appears a little later in Stephen's thoughts about the form of forms, unchanging under changing externals. In *Finnegans Wake* the relations of outer and inner appear more elaborately in the themes of clothing and the tailor.

"Having reprimed his repeater and resiteroomed his timespiece His Revenances, with still a life or two to spare for the space of his occupancy of a world at a time," speaks of the "mythical habiliments of Our Farfar and Arthor of our doyne." His Revenances' allusions to time-space and to repeating the cycle make it clear that Earwicker's clothing is his manifestation in time and space. After Our Farfar has risen from his burial under the lake and gone cycling off in fresh disguise, they find his clothing on the shore. Joyce mentions this and carefully catalogues Earwicker's clothing throughout the book because each change of clothing is an incarnation.

The tailor who cuts the coat, adapting it to any shape and style, also weaves the cloth. "Wovens weard" or what he weaves is Anglo-Saxon destiny. The tailor, who reappears throughout *Finnegans Wake,* is God or Adam, the "first breachesmaker." But he is also the artist or H. C. Earwicker. In the eleventh chapter, the scene in his pub, the song of reappearing John Peel with his coat so gray introduces the legend of the tailor and the sailor. Like the legend of the Prankquean, to which it is parallel, "the baffling yarn" is circular. Three times the Norwegian captain sails away and returns to quarrel with the tailor. This Viconian myth, dreamed during the time of deepest sleep, is many-leveled and unusually obscure. While in the pub, we are all at sea. But it is plain that Earwicker is both tailor and sailor, or, like any man, creator and rover. He weaves his destiny, cuts his coat, wears it, and refuses to pay. On his third visit, the Norwegian captain, trapped by the tailor's daughter, marries her. Tailor and rover are reconciled by marriage. The ball at the Tailors' Hall is at once the celebration of the captain's wedding and his wake.

Elsewhere, Earwicker, the tailor, appears as "Tawfulsdreck" and, since as publican he always bangs the shutter clup, he reappears as "shutter reshottus." *Sartor Resartus,* evoked by these allusions, is Carlyle's philosophy of clothes. This idealistic volume seems to have fascinated Joyce. He parodied it in the hospital scene of *Ulysses,* and made Mrs. Bloom the image of the "Everlasting Yea."

Clothing, says Carlyle, is everything external: the flesh, religion, society, the universe, and time and space. All these are the manifestations or clothes of reality. The spirit, weaving matter, manifests itself. Everything we see is the garment of the invisible. Beneath our externals resides the "divine Me," which reappears in *Finnegans Wake* as the "naked I." After discussing the clothing of Adam and the revival of the Phoenix, Carlyle recommends the annihilation of time and space. Joyce was not a transcendentalist, but, hunting parallels for his metaphors, he found excellent use for this Germanic philosopher.

Carlyle took his metaphor of clothes from Swift's *Tale of a Tub,* the story of Peter, Jack, and Martin, who, having inherited clothes from their father, change them by a liberal interpretation of his will to suit the fashion. By clothes, of course, Swift intended the externals of worship, and by the three sons he meant the churches of Rome, Geneva, and Canterbury. Swift was one of Joyce's heroes, and *The Tale of a Tub* was among his favorite books. The story of father and sons fitted the scheme of Joyce's family, while the metaphor of clothing proved another parallel in his theme of inner and outer. It is not surprising that among the hundreds of allusions to *The Tale of a Tub* during the course of *Finnegans Wake* there should be a "padderjagmartin" suit. "Behose our handmades for the lured," a parody of the Angelus, combines the themes of clothing and worship in the manner of Swift. And Shem, in the guise of Swift, is Mr. O'Shem the Draper.

Even the two washerwomen by the river Liffey belong to the theme of clothing. By washing dirty clothes, they renew the cycle. "Wring out the clothes!" they say, "Wring in the dew." Even the letter in the dump belongs to the theme; for it has an envelope. In his analysis, the professor pays particular attention to the outer husk or clothing of this document. To neglect its externals of time and space, he says, would be as hurtful to sound sense as to imagine a clothed body naked.

His concern with time and space reflects Joyce's concern with the physical world. As Stephen walks the changing beach, which symbolizes the flux of nature, he thinks of the "ineluctable modality" of the visible and of the audible. These definitions of space and time occupy him for "a very short space of time through very short times of space," as he walks into eternity perhaps. His time and space are those of the philosopher, but in the next to the last chapter of *Ulysses* time and space are those of the nineteenth-century physicist. This chapter takes the form of a scientific catechism. The cold questions and their cold exact answers, reducing reality to force and matter, project the inhumanity of science. Yet in this parody of scientific literature Joyce tells a human story about Bloom and Stephen:

> What, reduced to their simplest reciprocal form, were Bloom's thoughts about Stephen's thoughts about Bloom and Bloom's thoughts about Stephen's thoughts about Bloom's thoughts about Stephen?
> He thought that he thought that he was a jew whereas he knew that he knew that he knew that he was not.

The language is precise; but by making it extreme, Joyce achieved the grotesque. This humor is the difference between his language of science and the language of science. As Rabelaisian scientist, Joyce also observes Bloom and Mrs. Bloom: "She disliked umbrella with rain, he liked woman with umbrella, she disliked new hat with rain, he liked woman with new hat, he bought new hat with rain, she carried umbrella with new hat." In similar language Joyce expresses the conflict and reconciliation of other opposites. Uniting with each other, scientific Bloom and artistic Stephen become Stoom and Blephen.

When these reconciled opposites leave the house, they contemplate the universe. The illimitable vastness of interstellar space, the remoteness of the stars, and the inevitability of their motion give the observers a sense of man's insignificance. It was Joyce's purpose to place his Dubliners in the Newtonian universe, and by appropriate language to present the meaningless together with a human meaning. He brilliantly succeeded. This chapter of abstract relationships, either logical or mathematical, which resolves all human things into their physical equivalents without value or feeling, was Joyce's favorite. It is perhaps the funniest and the most moving chapter in all the book.

Joyce mentions Newton many times in *Finnegans Wake,* but this book presents the post-Newtonian universe of Einstein and Planck. References to Einstein make it clear that Joyce's "whorled without aimed" is that of twentieth-century physics. Self-contained, limited, curving back upon itself, *Finnegans Wake* is a multi-dimensional symbol of space-time.

Joyce was familiar with the work of Whitehead and Eddington, and he liked J. W. Dunne, whose serial time allows an observer in the fourth or fifth dimension to see past, present, and future simultaneously. Of the several references to Dunne in *Finnegans Wake,* this one, in which his idea of serial time is combined with Eddington's expanding universe, is perhaps the richest: all things, says Joyce, are "solarsystemised, seriolcosmically, in a more and more almightily expanding universe under one . . . original sun." Original sin, creation, and the family pattern easily combine with the "multimathematical immaterialites" of the new physics; for the cycle is "tetradomational" and in *Finnegans Wake* the four dimensions are at home.

The probable destruction of Earwicker is presented in physical terms. As his "moletons" escape with his "mubcules," Joyce foresaw the "abnihilisation of the etym." Atomic fission involves the collapse of the etym or the word; and the word means creation, humanity, and art. Following this dismal prospect, in the same paragraph, there are references to Coventry and Honolulu. It must be remembered that *Finnegans Wake* was published in 1939. Maybe this combination of Coventry, Pearl Harbor, and the atom bomb is no more than accident uniting with common sense. But Joyce, the master of cycles and hence of present, past, and future, used to joke about his prophetic powers.

Joyce's space-time continuum implies not only the union of space and time but the conflict of these opposites. The Cad in the Park introduces the theme of time. "What time is it?" he asks, and this enormous question echoes through *Finnegans Wake* as "Quote awhore" or "Let thor be horlog." If the Cad stands for time, Earwicker must stand for space, and their identity for space-time. But the quarrel of Shem and Shaun, which is also the quarrel of time and space, is easier to follow.

As unchanging stone, Shaun is space, and as changing elm, Shem is time. As the Ondt, Shaun defends space against the Gracehoper's time. In the sixth chapter, the dime-cash or time-space problem is the subject of Professor Jones, that eminent "spatialist." Attacking Bitchson (Bergson) and Winestain (Einstein), he disposes of the quantum theory, and, refuting Lévy-Bruhl, who also stands for time, he takes his stand with the "postvortex" school of Wyndham Lewis. *"Spice and Westend Woman"* recalls Wyndham Lewis' *Time and Western Man,* a neo-classical book, which, defending space, attacks Joyce and the romantic Bergsonists for adherence to the cult of time. To make himself clear to those of mean capacity Professor Jones embodies his neo-classical defense of space in the fable of the Mookse and the Gripes. From "Eins within a space," at the beginning, this fable proceeds through parsecs or units of space; but in the end only time and the river remain. Feeling dissatisfied with this ending, the professor reopens the question of time and space in the history of Burrus and Caseous. In these quarrels Joyce, who might seem to take his place with romantic Shem, has no favorites; for in their inevitable reconciliation Shem and Shaun or time and space are space-time.

Earwicker, the union of the twins, is a "tesseract" or a four-dimensional solid. Since an object of this kind is a mathematical concept and such concepts fit any physical things to which we want to assign them, we may think of the fourth dimension as time. It is likely that Joyce had time in mind as one of Earwicker's dimensions. As a tesseract, Earwicker is an event in space-time.

Bloom is a three-dimensional solid. That is why he stands out from the two-dimensional people who infest the pages of most novels. Three-dimensional Bloom necessarily exists at one time or another. But Earwicker in many bodies and in many places exists at all times. That is how he differs from Bloom and why it is more difficult to think of him. We cannot judge Earwicker by the standards we apply to characters in common novels or even by the standards we must invent for Bloom. Earwicker is concrete, yet he evades our habitual categories, and, although abstract, he evades our logic. "Where are we at all? and whenabouts in the name of space? . . . I fail to say." Successfully created, Earwicker is alive and moving and changing. He is something new in literature, and tesseract is as good a word for him as any.

Time calls for reconciliation with eternity, its opposite. Writers of our time, immersed in temporal flux, have been preoccupied with eternity. Some of them, like Aldous Huxley and T. S. Eliot, have attempted to exchange the cycle of time for the still point at the center. Eliot's *Four Quartets,* with its wheels and point, is an example of this attempt; and everybody knows how Huxley is stopping time in Hollywood. We have seen how Virginia Woolf, sunk deep in flux, made *To the Lighthouse* a quest for eternity.

Unlike these writers who, in need of something to depend upon, have tried to proceed from the relativity of time to an absolute outside it, Bergson found his absolute in time and so did Proust. Bergson found all reality and the absolute in the flow of consciousness, and Proust found them in memory and the relationship of past and present.

Like Bergson and Proust in this one respect, Joyce found the absolute in time and thereby reconciled it with eternity. He found eternity in the historical pattern, the family, and man. Above all these, he found eternity in art. The work of art, in which all things are reconciled, is an image of the absolute, as time, according to Nicholas of Cusa, is an image of the eternal. Formal, complete, at once in time and out of it, *Finnegans Wake* is a symbol of eternity. Existing "at no spatial time," it includes all cyclewheeling history. Earwicker, the human, godlike insect in his pub, proceeds from the void to fill it with the creative word: "In the buginning is the woid."

CHAPTER FOUR

MYTH AND SYMBOL

STEPHEN DEDALUS is fascinated by "suck," the word for water down a drain in the Wicklow Hotel. For more curious words he ransacks Skeat's *Etymological Dictionary,* adds them to his treasure house, and, taking them out, repeats them again and again. Although Stephen agrees that words are receptacles for thought, they acquire for him another value. Becoming intercessors, they stand between himself and reality. Through their agency alone he has "glimpses of the real world about him." Words do more than reveal that reality. They create it, and, as if God's compasses, draw significant form.

Like Rabelais, Joyce made grotesque catalogues of words. Like Nashe and Shakespeare, enamored of words in the age of discovery, he delighted in abundance. He called Shakespeare, whom he admired less as playwright than as poet, a "lord of language," richer than Dante and better to have on a desert island. Detesting "vague words for a vague emotion," he admired the precision of Flaubert. The Male Brutes who appear before unmanned Mr. Bloom in the brothel have only one thing to say. "Good!" they say. That is the *mot juste.* When the printers objected to the word "bloody" in the manuscript of *Dubliners,* Joyce replied that bloody is the one word in the language that can create the effect he wanted.

As he admired the words of other artists, so he exulted in his own command of what he considered the greatest of powers. To Eugene Jolas he announced: "I can do anything with language."

His study of archaic language and his notes on living language in street or pub had made him master of all verbal effects from the divine speech of thunder to "lowquacity." The words "Sechse-läuten" and "lebensquatsch," which occur throughout *Finnegans Wake,* are examples of both kinds. Sechseläuten is the spring festival of Zürich, and lebensquatsch or life's muddle is the interpretation by a Zürich waitress of Joyce's demand for lemon squash. He once told Frank Budgen that he had been working all day at two sentences of *Ulysses:* "Perfume of embraces all him assailed. With hungered flesh obscurely, he mutely craved to adore." When asked if he was seeking the *mot juste,* Joyce replied that he had the words already. What he wanted was a suitable order.

He composed a novel as great poets compose their poems. Under his hand all the resources of word, rhythm, and tone conspired to create intricate beauty. His novels are more like poems or symphonies or statues than like ordinary novels. Maybe they are not novels at all but works of their own kind like *Tristram Shandy* or *Gargantua,* which we call novels for want of a word for them. We must approach Joyce's greater works as we would a poem or a symphony. That reader who read *Ulysses* as if it were a common thing would be disappointed.

According to Ernst Cassirer's *Language and Myth,* words, which precede things in our minds, are the only way of knowing things. It is only after naming a thing that we control it. Therefore primitive men confused words with things, and, attributing magic power to words, used them for ritual or incantation. Since the power of the real thing was contained in its name, the word, as the power of powers, became God or His source or His creative instrument, and the agent for transforming chaos into cosmos. From this holy origin the word developed into a sign or symbol for something else, and, divested of potency in modern times, became a convenience. But the artist, recovering the ancient veneration of the word, recovers something of its potency. He uses it with reverence but without the limitations that surrounded his ancestors. What was once the means of practical magic becomes through his conscious control the means of aesthetic magic. Unlike a savage, the artist knows the word as the mind's revelation and the revelation of external reality.

What is true of the word is true of myth. Myth and language, Cassirer says, have a common origin in metaphor or analogy. Word, myth, and metaphor, coming from man's own being, are not imitations of nature. Each of them is a way of conceiving it, and each is a form of expression. What these expressive forms say cannot be said in terms of other things; for each of these forms gives its own insight into reality. Joyce, the master of words and analogies, was foremost among those who, reviving myth, have used its insights for modern art.

Ulysses is modelled more or less loosely upon an ancient myth. Joyce's Homeric parallel, as it is called, was the first of his devices to become known. Joyce told Valery Larbaud, who told the world; and Stuart Gilbert gave more than enough weight to the details. We know, therefore, that each of Joyce's main characters corresponds to one of Homer's. Bloom is Ulysses, Stephen is Telemachus, and Mrs. Bloom, who stays at home with the suitors, is Penelope. Her concern with metempsychosis supports the Homeric parallel by suggesting that Joyce's characters are the reincarnation of Homer's. Like the *Odyssey, Ulysses* is divided into three parts: the hunt of Telemachus for his father, the wanderings of Odysseus, and the return to Ithaca. Each episode of *Ulysses* corresponds to an episode of the *Odyssey*. But these episodes do not occur in the original order, for other than Homeric considerations helped to determine Joyce's structure. As he used Vico for *Finnegans Wake,* so for *Ulysses* he used Homer. To some extent structural devices, both Vico and Homer were of more use as expressive analogies. By references and hints, that are sometimes grotesque or trivial in character, Joyce suggests Homer. It is Homer's function to suggest in turn the central themes of *Ulysses*.

When the Citizen in Barney Kiernan's pub throws the biscuit tin at Mr. Bloom, he is parodying the Cyclops, but the Cyclops supports Joyce's point about Irish nationalism. Mr. Bloom's cigar, that corresponds to the stake with which Odysseus blinded the one-eyed giant, typifies Joyce's way of suggesting this reciprocal relationship between the ancient world and Dublin. "You don't grasp my point," says Homeric Mr. Bloom. Gerty Mac-Dowell and Nausicaa, those lovely seaside girls, help each other on their beaches to confirm the nature of woman. Metaphors of wind and all the winds of rhetoric make the newspaper office as windy as the home of Aeolus and our world.

Sometimes Joyce's characters play double parts. Mrs. Bloom, as both Penelope and Calypso, brings her husband home while keeping him abroad. In the fourth chapter, Calypso is symbolized by the picture Mr. Bloom has cut out from *Photo Bits,* but in the picture of that nymph he sees Mrs. Bloom. The ancient mariner in the cabman's shelter is a surrogate for Mr. Bloom. As Odysseus tells lies to Eumaeus about his voyages, so the dubious sailor tells lies to the belated company. Buck Mulligan, the "usurper" of the first chapter, is one of the suitors who keep Telemachus from his heritage and waste his substance. Yet Mulligan is one of the few in Dublin who have not enjoyed Mrs. Bloom.

In the third chapter, where the shifting sands suggest Proteus, Stephen is not only Telemachus searching the flux for a father but he is Menelaus as well, attempting to hold slippery reality in his hands. Change is symbolized by more than sand and tide. Words change, as every philologist knows, and all other things, assuming disguises, are "clutched at, gone, not here." The wonderful dog, trotting on twinkling shanks at the lacefringe of the tide, parodies the shapes of Proteus. A hare, a buck, a bear, a wolf, a calf, and a panther by turns, the dog at last sniffs rapidly "like a dog." The owners of this dog seem gypsies because Proteus is Egyptian. Stephen's changing mind passes from gypsies and Egyptians to gypsy-words:

> White thy fambles, red thy gan
> And thy quarrons dainty is.

These words, which, when looked up, are not half so bad as they sound, are by Richard Head, whose strange seventeenth-century verses invite Stephen to compose verses of his own. "Here. Put a pin in that chap," he says in the endeavor to fix Protean flux by art.

The "old chap picking his tootles" in the Burton restaurant, where Mr. Bloom goes in hope of food, suggests the cannibalism of Homer's Laestrygonians, and so does the limerick about the reverend Mr. MacTrigger, the missionary had by his flock for lunch. The man-eating Laestrygonians themselves, descending from their cliffs upon the black ships of Odysseus, are represented by the gulls, swooping from their heights about Anna Liffey to pounce on Mr. Bloom's Banbury cakes. For the curious ways in which Joyce recalls Scylla and Charybdis and other Homeric episodes one may consult Stuart Gilbert and Frank Budgen.

Victor Bérard's theory about the Semitic origins of the *Odyssey* increased, for Joyce, the likeness of Odysseus and Mr. Bloom. Not, of course, that Odysseus was a Jew, but he is the hero of a more or less Phoenician document in which a Jew could feel at home or away from it. "Jewgreek is greekjew. Extremes meet," says Lynch in the Circe episode or the scene in Bella Cohen's brothel. To strengthen the parallel Joyce also compares Bloom with those other restless Semites Sinbad the Sailor and the Wandering Jew.

Although an extraordinary linguist, Joyce knew little Greek —as we might expect of one who specialized in patristic Latin and modern languages. "*Oinopa ponton*" from the *Odyssey* and "polyfizzyboisterous seas" from the *Iliad* are embedded in *Ulysses* and *Finnegans Wake,* but these are the most familiar of Homeric tags. Buck Mulligan's "*thalatta*" is not Homeric Greek. There is enough of Homer around, however, to keep the attentive reader aware that in some sense *Ulysses* is a modern version of an ancient myth. To find in what sense *Ulysses* is a myth we must define myth.

Myth is the most difficult thing in the world. One man's definition contradicts another's, but most definers agree that since myth is pre-logical, it all but evades our thought. Many with whom Joyce was familiar—Vico, Frazer, Jung, and Lévy-Bruhl —had theories about myth. Let us consider what it is they thought.

According to Vico, myth is a primitive way of knowing. Before man became capable of generalizing, he saw things through the imagination. Poetry, the language of imagination, preceded prose, the language of reason. By myth and metaphor early man, incapable of logic, conceived and described reality as best he could. Myth is reality as it appears to the primitive mind. It is poetic allegory, corresponding to external reality but distorting it. Serious in intention, bizarre because a product of an infantile consciousness, myth is not philosophy, as Plato supposed, but early man's notion of his own history. By the analysis of myth and metaphor we can recover this ancient state of mind and something of man's past. Mythical heroes are not individuals but collective types. Innocent of abstraction, the Greeks personified their ideas of prudence in the figure of Odysseus. Even Homer, who, judging by his text, lived at many times in many places, is another invention of the ancient mind. Vico's idea of myth as history is generally dismissed under the name of euhemerism, but there is much in what he says about the poetic imagination.

In the late nineteenth century, mythologists thought myth an allegory of the weather, of the seasons, or of the sun and moon. *"Was Jesus a Sun Myth?"* is among the world's twelve worst books listed in the Circe episode of *Ulysses*. This may indicate Joyce's opinion of these mythologists. If, however, we may judge by references to Frazer's dying and reborn gods in *Finnegans Wake,* Joyce accepted Frazer's idea of myth. To Frazer, myth represents the seasonal cycle of fertility, death, and renewed fertility.

Freud did not say much about myth, but his followers said plenty. Karl Abraham said myth is a dream of the race as dream is a myth of the individual. Making more of this Freudian confusion of myth with dream, Otto Rank said that myth-makers invested the mythical hero with their own infantile history. The true hero of myth is the infant's ego in revolt against father. All myth, or almost all, is a symbolic projection of the Oedipus complex. In expressing his own unconscious, the myth-maker expressed that of other men, thereby acquiring social importance. While the manifest level of myth distracts men, the latent holds them to the chimney corner. Fairy tales, which Germanic peoples boast in greater variety, proved even more attractive to Freudians.

They paid particular attention to those fairy tales that concern the third son. But in these as in all other things they found the same thing.

To Jung, once a Freudian but now his own master, myth is also symbolic. Never to be taken literally or historically, myth is dream-fantasy, which, like the dreams of modern man, is at once archaic and infantile. Myth and dream alike summon archetypes from the collective unconscious.

As Jung himself noticed, Lévy-Bruhl's collective representations are not unlike archetypes. But Lévy-Bruhl insists upon social significance. Agreeing that the primitive mind is childish and illogical, he finds this mind projecting its emotions in collective symbols, which are neither explanations of nature nor concepts. Myth and ritual, the chief among these symbols, are expressive and unifying devices. Celebrating their own immanent power, they assure the solidarity of the group. Throughout his book on the mental functions of savages, Lévy-Bruhl quarrels pedantically with Frazer. It is for this reason perhaps that Joyce made Lévy-Bruhl a pedant in *Finnegans Wake* and the subject of Professor Jones' pedantic digressions.

Bronislaw Malinowski was Frazer's disciple. But as a field-anthropologist, who lived with myth-makers, Malinowski advanced a little beyond his master. After dismissing the psychoanalytic, the historical, and the allegorical interpretations of myth, he defined it. Far from being symbolic, he says in *Myth in Primitive Psychology,* myth is literal and useful. Its function is not explanatory or expressive but cultural. Myth is a narrative, which, satisfying deep religious, moral or social needs, sanctions ritual, contains practical rules for guidance, and constitutes a social charter. Justifying conduct by precedent, connecting the present with the past and with the supernatural, myth strengthens tradition while uniting the community. It furnishes meaning, place, and hope. Since this cultural device is always a narrative, it has literary aspects which may develop into epic or drama. Such developments, however, are none of his business. He makes it clear that he has Melanesians in mind and not the literate Greeks, to whom, for all he knows, Freud's follies may apply.

It may be possible to reconcile these discouraging differences of opinion, especially those of the psychoanalysts and the anthropologists, and to arrive at a workable definition. Since the psychoanalysts are concerned with the individual and the anthropologists with society, there could be less contradiction between their ideas than they think. European literary myth, which is what we are after, may serve individual and social purposes at once. Expressing the individual, it may unite the group. Here is a composite definition, which, although incomplete and doing justice to neither side, seems as good as any: Myth is a dreamlike narrative in which the individual's central concerns are united with society, time, and the universe. Both expression and sanction, it organizes experience, uniting fact with imagination, the conscious with the unconscious, the present with the past, man with nature, and the individual with the group. It gives values to reality and makes one feel at home. Allusions to the *Odyssey* do not make *Ulysses* mythical. *Ulysses* is mythical because it is a narrative which, while uniting Joyce with tradition, projects his central concerns.

Joyce considered Homer's myth the complete expression of man. In the departure of a family man from his home and in his return Joyce saw everybody's pattern. By adapting this general pattern to his own purposes, Joyce provided support for himself. Lonely and eccentric, he could feel one with mankind. His exile seemed only a departure to be followed by return. Away from home, he could feel at home. In the hunt of Telemachus for his father, Joyce found sanction for himself as artist. Telemachus can represent not only man's search for social support but the artist's search for humanity. Finding his father, Telemachus fulfills the wish of every man and every artist. Exile, home, humanity, and art, Joyce's concerns, found expression in Homer's *Odyssey*.

But the Homeric pattern is only one level of the narrative Joyce composed. Another level is the Christian pattern. As we have seen, Bloom is not only Odysseus but Jesus-God. These traditional levels, however, are less important than the main level of Joyce's myth: the story of Stephen Dedalus and Mr. Bloom in Dublin or the present, the particular, and the personal. *Ulysses* is a narrative composition of three levels, to which, by allusion,

Joyce added others of less importance. His myth is not the *Odyssey* but *Ulysses*.

Stephen had served Joyce in an earlier myth. *A Portrait of the Artist* embodies the myth of Daedalus. Finding expression for himself in the eighth book of *Metamorphoses,* Joyce connected Ovid's myth with personal history. References to the fabulous artificer throughout *A Portrait of the Artist* and in *Ulysses,* before its climax, justify exile and explain frustration. The myth of Stephen and Daedalus, projecting Joyce's quarrel with society, expressed his conditon and his desire. This composite myth united him with other exiles. All artists of the past century, or all whom he admired, composed a group in which, by no means least, he took his place. Any tradition was comforting. But to express fulfillment he had to exchange a parallel no longer adequate for that of Telemachus and Odysseus.

As the artist, ill at ease apart from society, finds justification in myth, society, feeling guilt for its treatment of the artist, finds similar justification. W. S. Gilbert's *Patience,* or the myth of the artist in reverse, defends Philistine contempt of art and sanctions exile. The artist is exiled because he is a sham. For a time Bunthorne can fool the ladies. But, finding him out, they turn with rewards to Archibald, who not only puts on commonplace pants but writes commonplace verses and will, no doubt, write books of the month. They turn also to heavy dragoons, but that is only natural. This opera, revived from time to time to support our ritual, delights us with music and, like all myths, with truth.

In the Circe or brothel episode of *Ulysses,* Stephen says, "The rite is the poet's rest." Joyce's support of the artist's ritual continues through the first half of *Finnegans Wake* in the story of exiled Shem. But, becoming one with his social brother, Shem takes his place in a larger tradition than that of exile. Becoming one with mankind, he takes his place in time. *Finnegans Wake* is the myth of eternal history. Joyce's narrative of the Earwicker family in the cycles of time sanctions humanity. Uniting the temporal and the eternal, the unconscious and the conscious, the individual and the universal, and all other opposites, it is perhaps the most comprehensive of myths.

Joyce built his earlier myths upon a foundation of ancient myth. The foundation of *Finnegans Wake* is philosophical. *Finnegans Wake* is not myth because it embodies Vico's cycles or Bruno's contraries but because it projects by narrative Joyce's central concerns and those of other men. In the course of this narrative he alludes to all the myths, legends, and fairy tales of the world: Leda and the Swan, Cinderella, Mutt and Jeff. Such parallels give richness and depth to the narrative. The sweet vision of the twenty-eight girls is projected as a fairy tale of Lady Shortbred in her Sundae dress and of Prince Le Monade, who serves not only as lemonade in this candied fantasy but as Bruno's monad or elementary form. The mythical stories of the Prankquean and of the Norwegian captain, both of whom go and return three times, are original variations on an old pattern. Implying death and birth again, most great myths are cyclical. *Finnegans Wake* is in the great tradition.

A myth composed by a modern artist, however, is different from ancient myth. More conscious for one thing, and more private for another, modern myth seems more elaborate and contrived than myths of the past. It was in part to remedy this defect that Joyce used old myths for new narratives. Familiar myth, moreover, guarantees a public level for new myth.

A measure of the difference between Joyce and the primitive myth-maker is provided by Joyce's attitude. The combination of heroic Odysseus with bourgeois Mr. Bloom, of Nausicaa with Gerty MacDowell, or of Daedalus with Stephen is not without ironic purpose or effect. The primitive mind is innocent of irony. At best, whether ironic or solemn, the modern myth is pseudo-myth. But its function for the maker is identical with that of ancient myth. And if, like Joyce's myths, the modern myth has a public level, it can do for us what myths did for our ancestors. *Ulysses* and *Finnegans Wake* have a social function; for modern man needs to be assured of his humanity.

Joyce was but one of many who revived old myths in order to make new ones. Yeats drew upon Leda and the Swan and Dove and Virgin to furnish the great wheel of history, and all reviving gods attend its revolutions. D. H. Lawrence drew upon Genesis, the fantasies of Wagner, and the myths of ancient Mexico for his novels. These narratives of death and rebirth contain a private level—not altogether without social meaning—of the little black, horse-loving proletarian who always runs off with the duchess. And in *The Waste Land* Eliot combined the quest for the Grail and the resurrection of Frazer's gods with a suggested narrative of modern London. Overtones of Dante and the Christian myth found more emphatic, but still indirect, expression in *Four Quartets,* where cycles of time lead us to the point of eternity. These works are like Joyce's works in kind. Not all good literature of our time is myth, but much of it seems to be or, at least, to be trying to be.

Man needs his myth. But our society, unlike some of its predecessors, has no common myth. In its place are the competing myths of Marx, Rome, and free enterprise. While tractor, Virgin, and icebox, the symbols of these contenders, clamor for allegiance, many people find themselves unable to give it. For expressing their needs some of them invent private myths; and myth, a preservative against confusion, increases it. Yet in the hands of an artist a more or less private myth may express the age as none of our public myths has done. T. S. Eliot, in his essay on *Ulysses* and myth, finds Joyce giving order, shape, and significance to our confusion. Joyce's myth, he says, is "the most important expression" that our age has found, and, what is more, his mythical method is a way of "making the modern world possible for art."

Our world, as Eliot implies, has become impossible or almost impossible for art because we have come to accept fact and the evidence of our senses as total reality. Accepting fact as a gift to our senses, we forget that there may be other realities and several ways to them. Bacon declared the independence of fact and Hobbes defined its language. Since their time all other realities and languages have gone into retirement and our world has become a literal thing. Metaphor and other imaginative ways have seemed little more than decorations. Instead of uniting the worlds of imagination and fact as Shakespeare's language had done, the language of the eighteenth century separated into two kinds. The central language, expresssing fact, became increasingly sterile. Decorative language, separated from fact, lost its substance. Neither language could express the whole of man or his reality. Since reality depends upon its language, there was little place for religion or art.

Lamenting the separation of fact and value, Eliot named it "the dissociation of sensibility." No other diagnosis of our trouble is half so famous; for no other phrase more successfully unites truth and jargon. By his poetry Eliot united the dissociated worlds, and by his propaganda he cemented them together. Before Eliot's time, Yeats had tried to restore dead metaphor to life by adventures in the occult world to which imagination had retired. Indeed, since the time of Blake, poets, rebelling against a meaningless world of fact, had occupied their exile from factual society by affirming the imaginative way to truth. Whitehead sees the romantic movement as a protest in behalf of value. In this long endeavor to unite two worlds of reality, myth has been no less important than metaphor; for by its nature myth is an agent of unity. In Joyce's myth Eliot saw imagination joining fact and metaphysics joining physics in their ancient fellowship.

Far from being the only way to reality, science is but one of many ways. Myth, ritual, and the several arts are equally valid ways of conceiving ourselves and what surrounds us. Giving insights of equal importance, they also express us and represent our reality. Cassirer calls them "symbolic forms." And in *Philosophy in a New Key,* Susanne Langer, who follows Cassirer in identifying myth and symbol, calls symbols the central concern of philosophers, who see in them the door to knowledge and its key. Giving us our knowledge, symbols organize it.

Myth may be a symbolic form but defining symbol is easier than defining myth. Symbolism is presenting a concept by indirection or analogy. A symbol, in its lowest terms, is something that stands for something else. Commonly a sensuous image, it represents something too large, complex, unspeakable, or ideal for direct expression. Dante's rose, for example, suggests his heaven; and Einstein's formula suggests our universe. Although a non-mathematical symbol commonly resembles its object in some particulars, it differs in others. For this reason it is never literal like a description or a statement and never simple like a sign, which has one meaning alone. Proceeding by analogy from the known to the unknown and sometimes the unknowable, the symbol is a way of knowing.

Since a symbol reconciles two hitherto unrelated areas, it is a way of uniting. Jung calls it a mediator between the conscious and the unconscious and between all other pairs of opposites. The true symbol is many-sided and evocative. No interpretation, he says, can reach the end of what is endless nor can it exhaust the inexhaustible. His archetypes, he continues, are symbols, whereas Freud's so-called symbols are signs with single meanings. Not everybody would agree with Jung about Freud, but many poets agree with him about the nature of the symbol. Yeats tried to unify himself and his divided world by forms that express what nothing else expresses or can express.

Dante's rose is a symbolic form, and so is *The Divine Comedy* in which the rose has its place and function. The entire work of art expresses and presents what nothing else can express or present. Music, says Susanne Langer, is not feeling but what symbolizes the form of our feeling. Poetry is not thought but what symbolizes the form of our thought, and from thought's image comes our feeling. A poem is the harmony of sound, rhythm, and meaning. In "The Symbolism of Poetry" Yeats defines symbolic form:

> All sounds, all colours, all forms, either because of their pre-ordained energies or because of long association, evoke indefinable and yet precise emotions . . . and when sound, and colour, and form are in a musical relation, a beautiful relation to one another, they become as it were one sound, one colour, one form, and evoke an emotion that is made out of their distinct evocations and yet is one emotion.

In defining symbolic form and the expressive harmony of part and whole, Yeats had the symbolists of France in mind. The French symbolist movement, one of the principal expressions of romanticism, was the most effective protest against the world of fact.

The aim of these symbolists, who flourished in the last quarter of the nineteenth century, was, while counteracting their literal world by all that seemed its opposite, to create and present a better reality. In place of describing, explaining, and stating, as realists preferred to do, the symbolists suggested and evoked. Their reality, too complex and ideal for statement or description, found embodiment in concrete images or in harmonious interactions among images, rhythm, and sound. The physical world, retaining a functional value at least, afforded ways of saying what cannot be said. In short, they made symbolic forms as every artist does, but they differed from many artists in knowing what they were about and in writing manifestoes about it.

To Baudelaire, nature was little more than a repository of symbols for things beyond it or inside him or he knew not where. Since the symbol unites matter and spirit, inner and outer, time and eternity, correspondence seemed a better name for it. Baudelaire found this name in Swedenborg, who saw all things in heaven and earth and between them lines of influence. By the power of physical symbols seer or poet could call down parts of heaven or make the best of both worlds. In his famous sonnet "Correspondances," Baudelaire suggests not only the transcendental value of the symbol but finds it connecting the senses in such a way that he can feel colors, or hear smells, or taste Wagner's music. The odor of brown and red marigolds always sounded like the grave and profound tones of an oboe. Synesthesia or the confusion of the senses is only one power of the imagination, which, creating analogies and discovering symbols, evokes reality. Through "reciprocal analogy" alone the world acquires meaning and value.

Delighted by the mysterious charm of a full-rigged ship, he proclaimed man's need of complication, harmony, and design. He visited theaters in order to see the adorable chandeliers, more intricate and symmetrical than anything the stage could show. These symbols of art are symbolic forms. As for description, photography or copying nature in novels—such things are for democrats or Belgians.

Rimbaud, Verlaine, Mallarmé, and Maeterlinck, following

the master's teachings, created forms of their own. Not Swedenborg, but Cabalists and the students of Hermes Trismegistus gave
Rimbaud his knowledge of correspondences. It was he, he said,
who discovered the color of vowels and noted the inexpressible.
The wonderful poems in which he accomplished these things—
sometimes incantations, sometimes myths—are forms for discovering reality; and so are the symphonic indirections of Mallarmé,
the evocative music of Verlaine, and the exquisite silences of
Maeterlinck. These are the symbolists Joyce read.

In his essay on Mangan, Joyce mentions Baudelaire without
enthusiasm, but quotes him in *Finnegans Wake,* where he reappears among rivers and women as "boudeloire," a not inappropriate fusion of boudoir with mud of Loire. Mary Colum tells us
that Joyce had Baudelaire's "Correspondances" by heart. The
master's synesthesia or maybe that of Huysmans, with whom
Joyce was also familiar, seems to attend that moment in the
Eumaeus episode of *Ulysses* when Stephen "could hear, of course,
all kinds of words changing colour," responding to context as the
crabs of Ringsend to environment. The cries of birds in *A Portrait
of the Artist* seem as shrill to Stephen as threads of silken light.

Shortly after this synesthetic experience, he thinks of "black
vowels." In *Stephen Hero,* Stephen, after reading Rimbaud on the
colors and values of letters, proceeds to permute and combine his
vowels in order "to fix the most elusive of his moods." Under
Rimbaud's spell, he puts his verses together not word by word
but letter by letter. Oliver Gogarty, who is Buck Mulligan in
Ulysses, says that when he and Joyce lived together in the tower,
Joyce was always talking of Rimbaud, upon whose revolt, character, and language, he faithfully modelled his own. "Mithy-
phallic" in *Finnegans Wake* is the mythical resurrection of
Rimbaud's famous "ithyphallique."

Joyce's friends agree about his admiration of Verlaine. In
Stephen Hero Stephen uses the word "literature" as a term of
contempt for all mediocre writing. This is an echo of "Art
poétique," Verlaine's manifesto. To Joyce, in the essay on Mangan, Verlaine's songs, which seem as free and "remote from conscious purpose as rain that falls in a garden," are "the rhythmic

speech of an emotion otherwise incommunicable, at least so fitly." No Frenchman defined symbolism more fitly than this. While an undergraduate, Joyce translated poems by Verlaine as well as passages from Maeterlinck.

That Belgian received young Joyce's homage in *The Day of the Rabblement,* and in *Stephen Hero* Maeterlinck's *Intruder* seems so ineffable that Stephen is reluctant to talk about it to common men. In *Ulysses,* however, he listens quietly while A.E. and the librarian discuss Maeterlinck, Mallarmé, and Villiers de l'Isle Adam. Stephen's recollection of Gérard de Nerval, leading his lobster down the street by a bright blue ribbon, could come only from Arthur Symons' *Symbolist Movement in Literature.* It was Yeats, the symbolist, who introduced Joyce to Symons, the leading authority on French symbolism, and it was he who found a publisher for Joyce's poems. Joyce turned to these symbolists because they showed him ways of expressing what he wanted to express. Master of word and myth, he too was a symbolist, scorning the imitation of nature and constructing symbolic forms that give a deeper insight into nature than imitation can. To Frank Budgen, Joyce said, "I want the reader to understand always through suggestion rather than direct statement."

Like his French predecessors, Joyce was contemptuous of external realism, especially that of the naturalistic school, which, under Zola's management, celebrated fact by scientific method. Those critics who have praised or condemned Joyce's naturalism are mistaken. In *The Day of the Rabblement* Joyce finds George Moore, the first English naturalist, struggling in the backwater of French realism, a current unrelated to the future of art. It is true, however, that Moore's *Esther Waters,* condemned here, received Joyce's praise in later years as the "best novel of modern English life." But since no English novel of the nineteenth century seemed of the first order, this praise is not unqualified. In a letter Joyce expressed his fear that readers of *Dubliners* would call him the Irish Zola. Such outmoded realism, however, was no part of his aim.

Joyce exempted one realist from his general condemnation. Flaubert, the greatest artist among Balzac's followers, pleased

Joyce so thoroughly that he memorized whole pages. Not only the verbal elegance and precision of that master proved attractive, but the subjective method of *The Temptation of St. Anthony,* the ironic vision of *Bouvard and Pécuchet,* and the universality of *Madame Bovary.*

Since the naturalists tried to establish external reality, they were descriptive. Before perfecting his art, Joyce tried this method. The Dublin of *Dubliners* and its people are described. But almost abandoning description in *Ulysses* Joyce evoked place and people. He established his characters by what they say; and his places, named but not described, live in the minds of his characters. Yet no place is more solid than Joyce's Dublin and no characters are more substantial. Only a few parts of *Ulysses* contain description. During his walk along the beach, Stephen exercises his descriptive powers on what he sees and hears. Gerty MacDowell's scene, which concerns the eye, is suitably pictorial. The catalogue of externals in Mr. Bloom's parlor is not naturalistic but a parody of naturalism and its reduction to absurdity.

Joyce did not approach things directly like a naturalist but indirectly, through correspondence or analogy, as a symbolist. For correspondence he had no need of consulting Baudelaire or Rimbaud, for he was on familiar terms with their occult authorities. While thinking of correspondences on the steps of the library in *A Portrait of the Artist,* Stephen recalls Swedenborg and Cornelius Agrippa. Inspired by the rituals of Yeats' Michael Robartes, Stephen reads Joachim de Flora. These masters of correspondence joined William Blake, Pico della Mirandola, and Jakob Boehme in his mind. As Stephen walks the beach, thinking of externals and their relation to reality, externals seem "signatures of all things." This phrase from Boehme, the mystical alchemist, implies the doctrine of correspondence, upon which alchemy is founded, and the relationship of microcosm or man with macrocosm or the universe. In Mr. Bloom's kitchen, Stephen sees himself as "a conscious rational reagent between a micro and a macrocosm ineluctably constructed upon the incertitude of the void." This view of the correspondence of microcosm with macrocosm is called hermetic after Hermes Trismegistus, who,

in his *Emerald Tablet,* says, "Things below are as things above."
Joyce often mentioned Hermes and quoted him: "The tasks above
are as the flasks below, saith the emerald canticle of Hermes."
This passage from *Finnegans Wake* suggests a relationship between the pattern and the particulars of history or between the
creator and the vessels of his creation. In "the belowing things
ab ove," Hermes is almost lost in confusion with bulls and eggs;
for this passage occurs in the fable of the Mookse and the Gripes,
and the bull is papal. These allusions to hermetic correspondence
are not there to proclaim belief but to serve as correspondences
for points in the narrative.

Yeats, losing himself in alchemy and the Cabala, believed
in correspondence. This was also the central tenet of A.E. and the
other Theosophists, who crowded Dublin in Joyce's time. Joyce
appears to have been fascinated with A.E. as one is sometimes
fascinated with a repulsive thing. In *Ulysses,* A.E., "the master
mystic," appears as one of "that hermetic crowd, the opal hush
poets." As he passes along the street, talking of the transcendental octopus, or revolves in the whirlpool of mysticism, he is
absurd. Stephen often thinks of Mme Blavatsky, A.E.'s philosopher, and her curious beliefs. But Stephen's tone is always
cynical or jocular. Taking refuge from the occult whirlpool,
where A.E. revolves with Platonists and Quakers, Stephen shares
the rock of dogma with Aristotle, Loyola, and Aquinas. But that
reasonable man Mr. Bloom, avoiding the Charybdis of mysticism
and the Scylla of dogma, walks politely between them. Joyce, who
was no less reasonable, knew all that Theosophists know about
the pineal eye and the seven chakras of yoga. He knew as much
as Cabalists about the ineffable name. His four old men of
Finnegans Wake, who use an occult symbol to draw buried
memories from Yawn, are imitating Cabalistic Yeats. But whereas
occultists used such things for worship or magic, Joyce used them
for art. Correspondence served him as a literary method.

Joyce had a queer mind. He was always seeing analogies.
When he saw a Mookse, twenty parallels occurred to him. They
range in kind from Yardley's soap to the frog who would a-wooing
go. That is another reason why double or triple talk commended

itself to Joyce as his vehicle. When he thought of Odysseus, he thought of Mr. Bloom, Sinbad, Hanno, and six or seven other voyagers. When he read Vico, he saw correspondences with the family pattern. Joyce's work is an elaborate structure of analogies, parallels, or correspondences. All of them, corresponding to reality, present it.

Frenchmen and hermetists were not Joyce's only examples. Ibsen, who had seemed a sociologist to Shaw, seemed profounder than that to Joyce. With his eye on *A Doll's House,* Shaw found what he wanted and could find. Contemplating *The Wild Duck, The Master Builder,* and all the later plays, Joyce found "orchestral harmonies" and symbols. Nothing can be more mysterious or suggestive than a builder falling from his tower or a duck in the attic. Ibsen became Joyce's favorite. In Hauptmann, some of whose symbolic plays Joyce translated, he found Ibsen's successor.

Among older symbolists was Dante, whose four levels of meaning confirmed Joyce in his passion for complexity and multiple significance. There was also Phineas Fletcher, whose *Purple Island,* an allegory of the human body, delighted Joyce. Fletcher's identification of the organs with features of the landscape expresses the mediaeval belief in correspondence between microcosm and macrocosm. His elaborate metaphor, a way of knowing man and nature, is one of those ways of knowing that Bacon and Hobbes were at pains to destroy and that modern poets have been at pains to revive.

Eminent among these poets, Joyce used mediaeval correspondence in the symbols of man's body and his arts. Each of Mr. Bloom's chapters symbolizes an organ and an art. Stephen, who is incomplete, lacks organs, and Mrs. Bloom, as nature, lacks art. These symbols are formed by allusion and technique. In the Hades or cemetery episode, where the organ is the heart, Mr. Bloom thinks of pumps and the Sacred Heart. In the episode of the Wandering Rocks or the labyrinth, where the art is mechanics, there are a dynamo, a typewriter, Tom Rochford's strange machine, and the only motor-car of *Ulysses.* These references establish the city and perhaps the universe as a vast machine. The ruminative technique of the lunch-hour chapter suggests both Laestrygonians and the alimentary canal. Linking Homer's world with Dublin, man's body, and the arts, such correspondences present knowledge of mankind.

To his useful list of organs, arts, and Homeric parallels, Stuart Gilbert adds the symbols by which Joyce expressed the mood of each chapter and its color. The symbolism of color, if there at all, is probably French. Joyce mixed his schools of correspondence according to his needs. In his books the mediaeval system and the French work in harmony with the systems of Freud and Jung, about which it seems unnecessary to say more here.

As a sculptor in order to express his idea may make the buttocks larger or smaller than usual, or as a painter, like Picasso, may distort the natural form in order to create expressive form, so Joyce used distortion to make the symbol. The parodies throughout *Ulysses* distort nature to express it. Joyce's portrait of the Citizen in Barney Kiernan's pub consists of outrageous parodies and gigantic caricatures which, quarreling with the real speech of Dublin, compose a form to express the nationalist. Symbolic distortion does it better than Zola's realistic devices could.

Grotesque symbolic themes, linking distortion to distortion, are equally expressive. Of these the most fascinating is Plumtree's Potted Meat. While talking of Molly to M'Coy in the fifth chapter of *Ulysses,* Mr. Bloom sees this advertisement in the paper:

> What is home without
> Plumtree's Potted Meat?
> Incomplete.
> With it an abode of bliss.

As an advertising man, Mr. Bloom dislikes the form of this advertisement and its place beneath the obituaries, but it haunts him all that day. At its first appearance, the potted meat represents Mrs. Bloom, without whose flesh the home is incomplete. Recurring in the lunch-hour context as Paddy Dignam's potted meat, it symbolizes not only food but death and burial; for hungry

Mr. Bloom has just returned from burying Paddy. When Mr. Bloom comes home in the morning, he finds an empty pot of Plumtree's Potted Meat in the kitchen and some flakes of that dubious product in the bed upon the imprint of Boylan's form. Potted meat is now Boylan's enjoyment of Mrs. Bloom. Molly's home has been complete, but, furnished only with an empty pot, Mr. Bloom's is incomplete. Since Plumtree's trade-mark is a plum tree in a pot, potted meat corresponds to the plums of Stephen's parable of the plums and to the tree of life. Expanding from context to context, this symbol expresses life, death, love, and home.

Two weeks and three days before June 16, 1904, Mr. Bloom has been stung by a bee and treated for his wound by Dr. Dixon. Recollections of this bee-sting, throughout *Ulysses,* symbolize Mr. Bloom's sin against fertility and its punishment. These recollections culminate in the hospital scene, which, corresponding to Homer's Oxen of the Sun, presents that sin. It is Dr. Dixon who invites Mr. Bloom to the party in the hospital. Both of them recall the bee. In *Finnegans Wake* the bee reappears as a Freudian symbol in the context of the twenty-eight girls. As "iris riflers," the bees are buzzy about their combs.

Other symbols help to carry the major theme of fertility and infertility. There is, for example, the Gold Cup Race, which is both an actual race and a Freudian symbol. In this race, Sceptre, the phallic favorite, loses to Throwaway, the outsider, who represents infertility. The symbol of the race track in *Finnegans Wake* is at once Freudian and Viconian. Coming to mind throughout Bloom's day and changing with its context, the Child's murder case is another symbol of sterility. In the graveyard episode it refers to death, and in the maternity episode to contraception.

Continual allusions to cattle and their disorders establish the foot and mouth disease, the subject of Mr. Deasy's letter to the press, as a significant theme. In the maternity hospital, cattle serve as an obvious symbol of fertility, and foot and mouth disease, the trouble with cows, becomes a symbol of infertility and Dublin's distemper. That foot and mouth also function on a Freudian level (foot as male and mouth as female) corroborates their meaning in this context. As "bullockbefriending bard," Stephen champions fertility or art against the sterility around him.

The man in the brown macintosh is a more enigmatic symbol. First appearing as the thirteenth man in the cemetery, where he arouses Bloom's curiosity, he reappears in the streets of the Wandering Rocks and again, drinking Bovril, at the end of the maternity chapter. Bovril or the essence of fertile cows does little good. For when this mysterious figure reappears in the Circe episode, his raincoat symbolizes contraception or the sin against fertility. This meaning, however, escapes Mr. Bloom, who, at the end of his day, wonders "Who was M'Intosh?" He is not only a symbol of death but a symbol of what we cannot know.

Even *Chamber Music,* Joyce's first book of poems, is an example of symbolist indirection. These delicate, mannered poems seem trivial. Apparently extracting the final elegance from tradition, Joyce sings of love in the manner of the Elizabethans and of the poets of the eighteen-nineties. His love of Jonson, Shakespeare, Nashe, and the lutanists appears in *A Portrait of the Artist,* where he describes the composition of his earliest verses—villanelles for the most part, now lost to us except perhaps for those he attributes to Stephen. If we may judge by Stephen's poems, the loss of these early exercises was no misfortune. The sad melodious rhythms of *Chamber Music* and such words as "comedian capuchin" and "plenilune" prove that Verlaine and Dowson were among his models, while neatness and a reference to Mithridates recall Housman. The hand of early Yeats is obvious; but sometimes Joyce anticipates the hardness and precision of the later Yeats. Inversions and the poetic diction of the nineties fail to agree with syntactical felicities, daring rhymes, and modern-sounding assonance. On the whole, however, these songs, although pleasing enough and suitable for an Irish tenor, seem to justify their comparative neglect. Readers have complained that Joyce, who wrote poetry when he wrote prose, wrote verse when he tried poetry. Indeed, it is likely that if someone else had written *Chamber Music,* it would have been forgotten.

Since Joyce did write it, however, we can neither dismiss it lightly nor take it at its face value. We must remember that his mind was far from simple. A poem, he said, is deliberately made; and what Joyce made he made in his intricate image. Upon examination, these poems appear more malicious than tender and more realistic than fanciful. Some of the poems are what they seem to be, but in most of them, tone and matter quarrel with their manner. Joyce appears to be having fun with his formal measures.

His view of love is not what his metrical tradition implies. Stephen provides the necessary clue. In *Stephen Hero* he says that although he retains "feudal terminology" for his love poems, he is "compelled to express his love a little ironically. This suggestion of relativity, he said, mingling itself with so immune a passion is a modern note." He is speaking of the early exercises, but what he says applies to *Chamber Music*. Kept to the surface of these poems by their smooth perfection, we may miss what Joyce is saying: that love is illusory or inconstant and that love is death. The first poem makes this point. Playing on his Elizabethan instrument, love enters with "pale flowers" and "dark leaves." These Pre-Raphaelite decorations are not those of love but death. The metrical finality of the last stanza, modified by this meaning, becomes finality of another kind. But love as death, a familiar idea in literature, is the least of Joyce's incongruities. Poem XXXI, a charming song of the poet walking with his girl, seems conventional except for one line: "the bat flew from tree to tree." What is a bat doing in a love poem? And why, unlike a bat, does it flit from tree to tree? This bat is symbolic and so are the trees. They are men and the bat is woman, his girl in particular. This suggestion of the vampire gives another meaning to the sweetness of her smile and the softness of her kiss.

The bat became one of Joyce's recurrent symbols. In *A Portrait of the Artist* Stephen's girl and the peasant woman who invites Davin to stay the night are "batlike" souls. As Gerty MacDowell looks with longing at Mr. Bloom, a bat flits from its belfry and around them—as it flits again around the washerwomen by the river in *Finnegans Wake*. When Stephen composes a poem on the beach in the third chapter of *Ulysses,* his subject is the vampire. He is composing these verses in 1904, the year in which Joyce wrote *Chamber Music*. In 1897, Bram Stoker, a fellow Dubliner, had written *Dracula,* to which Joyce alludes in *Finnegans Wake*. His bat, like his bird, is commonly feminine, but bat and bird are sometimes symbols of the exiled artist, in whose nature, as in that of Shem, the feminine principle is strong. Daedalus flew; Swift is a kind of bird; but Sterne, Swift's twin in *Finnegans Wake,* means bottom.

That Joyce with indirection however elegant should call his girl a vampire while she kisses him is bad enough, but his references to her other natural functions are worse. A clue to their nature is afforded by the title of *Chamber Music,* which, as Joyce explains in *Ulysses,* is an indelicate pun. What on one level means formal elegance means reality at its most fundamental on another. Some poems of what Joyce was to call "shamebred music" are mellifluous in two senses. Mrs. Bloom on her pot, the "bright cascade" of Poulaphouca, and the two girls making water in the bushes were anticipated by the girls of *Chamber Music*. When in Poem VII Joyce's love in gay attire goes lightly among the apple-trees, it is not for nothing that she holds up her dress with dainty hand. Poem XXVI is more domestic:

> Thou leanest to the shell of night,
>   Dear lady, a divining ear.
> In that soft choiring of delight
>   What sound hath made thy heart to fear?
> Seemed it of rivers rushing forth
> From the grey deserts of the north?

For Joyce, the lutanist of love, as for Yeats, love had pitched his mansion in the place of excrement. The mad humor of Joyce's poems may seem indecorous or perverse, but it is probably no more than play with incompatibilities of form and matter and his first experiment with symbolism. For a man as self-centered as Joyce the danger of direct expression was sentimentality. It was partly to avoid this danger and partly to protect his soul while expressing it that he put on a kind of mask. Under its elegance and indecency he found the detachment that his later poems lack. The trouble with the poems in *Pomes Penyeach* is that they are direct, and Joyce's talent was for indirection.

By the time of *Ulysses* Joyce was using the technique of allusion and quotation made familiar by T. S. Eliot. Such references carry meanings from an old context to enrich the new, where they abide like radiant plums. The library scene, for example, begins with an allusion to *Wilhelm Meister*. This is not here by accident or for display but to suggest a comparison of Stephen's Hamlet with Wilhelm's and to suggest a comparison of Stephen with Goethe's adolescent. In the brothel scene, the Croppy Boy, whose tragedy Ben Dollard has sung in his base barreltone, appears before Stephen, and, with the rope around his neck, says: "Horhot ho hray ho rhother's hest." This strangulated attempt to say "And forgot to pray for my mother's rest," a line from the patriotic ballad, helps to establish the theme of Stephen's guilt. The references in *Finnegans Wake* to *A Royal Divorce,* a once famous play by W. G. Wills, suggest the correspondence of Earwicker and his girls to Napoleon and his.

Allusions take their place in a great variety of symbolic devices, ranging in kind from numbers, signs, and the one-to-one correspondences of allegory to symbols as vast as Mr. Bloom. But to talk of symbols in a work of art is not to talk of the work of art as symbol. Together with rhythm, sound, tone, and the relation of part to part, symbols of all kinds make a composite symbol. This symbolic form or the work itself has its own significance.

The aesthetic theory in *A Portrait of the Artist* is a definition of significant form. For beauty, says Aquinas, three things are required: wholeness, harmony, and radiance. Wholeness means that the work, selfbounded and selfcontained, is apprehended as one thing. After that, says Stephen,

> you pass from point to point, led by its formal lines; you apprehend it as balanced part against part within its limits; you feel the rhythm of its structure. . . . You apprehend it as complex, multiple, divisible, separable, made up of its parts, the result of its parts and their sum, harmonious.

Harmony is the relation of part to part and of the part to the whole. Radiance is not symbolic in the sense of corresponding to the ideal or the divine; but, as something peculiar to the work itself, it is symbolic in another sense. Like Gerard Manley Hopkins' "inscape," radiance is the "whatness" of wholeness and harmony or the significance of form.

In *Stephen Hero,* Stephen identifies radiance with epiphany. From the external appearance and the composite structure of the object, he says, its soul or whatness leaps out and the object "achieves its epiphany." Joyce satisfied his ecclesiastical temper by using ecclesiastical terms for his secular aesthetics. Like Aquinas' radiance, epiphany is an ecclesiastical term for symbolism. Epiphany means a showing-forth or, as Stephen defines it, "a sudden spiritual manifestation." While walking along Eccles Street, he hears a fragment of vulgar conversation. This trivial incident becomes for him the symbol of a spiritual state, and through his insight the incident finds its epiphany; for epiphany is not only the meaning of a symbol but the artist's apprehension of that meaning. In spite of Stephen's identification, radiance and epiphany are not identical. Whereas radiance is the property of art, epiphany may belong to any experience.

For Joyce, as for Baudelaire, common reality became a storehouse of symbols awaiting apprehension. "In every stray image of the streets," Stephen sees his girl's soul "manifest itself." Even the clock of the Ballast Office provides an epiphany as he tries "to pierce to the significant heart of everything." The supreme artist, he says, is one who can "disentangle the subtle soul of the image from its mesh of defining circumstances most exactly and 're-embody' it in artistic circumstances chosen as the most exact for it in its new office." His hell is a region where everything is obvious. The mere "literature" that he despises deals with external things. When he calls himself a classicist, he implies more than a regard for concreteness and limitation. Taking present things, the classicist so fashions them that he "may go beyond them to their meaning which is still unuttered."

Stephen plans a collection of significant trivialities. Many of these may be embedded in *A Portrait of the Artist:* the conversation of Stephen and his girl on the step of the tram, for example, and the girl wading at the beach. And it is likely that *Dubliners* resembles the collection that he planned. These stories of trivial events are not naturalistic. The naturalistic details that appear in them are in the service of symbolism. No stories achieve their effects more obliquely. That the sermon delivered by the Jesuit in "Grace" is more worldly than the business men to whom it is addressed is implied by the sermon, but never stated. The sentimentality and emptiness of the patriots in "Ivy Day in the Committee Room" are disclosed by a "pok" from a bottle, warming at the fire. In "Clay," which tells of a pathetic spinster at a Halloween party, the bowl of clay, symbolizing death, carries the meaning. These indirections culminate in "The Dead," the last, the subtlest, and the most masterly story. After the party and his wife's disclosures, Gabriel Conroy contemplates the decay of hearts, and, as the symbolic snow descends, becomes one with all the dead. A passage from one of Baudelaire's essays applies to *Dubliners:* "In certain almost supernatural states of soul the depth of life is revealed in ordinary everyday happenings. Ordinary life then becomes the Symbol." Oliver Gogarty thinks all the speeches of Buck Mulligan in *Ulysses* are "give-aways" or epiphanies. But Stephen's parable of the plums, which begins with "I have a vision too," is a better example.

In *Finnegans Wake,* as Earwicker's trousers fall, the analyst observes, "How culious an epiphany." But this showing-forth of the bottom is balanced by a showing-forth of the top in the speech of the Archdruid. That idealist, who pierces through the veil of externals to "the Ding hvad in idself id est," also speaks of epiphany. His "heupanepiphanal world" is the external world awaiting discovery by the artist, and heliotrope is seeing epiphanies. Joyce's works are more than containers of little epiphanies. *Ulysses* and *Finnegans Wake* are great epiphanies, disclosing their whatness and the whatness of reality. But this is only a fancier way of calling them significant forms.

Form, says Kenneth Burke, is the arousing and fulfilling of desires. By this he seems to mean the creating of tensions and their resolution. According to this idea, *Ulysses* is a formal triumph. The tensions of Stephen and Mr. Bloom, mounting separately throughout their day, unite at last and find common resolution. Although their tensions, which are also ours, occupy the narrative level, they are resolved on other levels—by the symbolic cup of cocoa and by Mrs. Bloom. She is not, as she might seem, a more or less irrelevant addition to the narrative nor is she there for her own sake. That she is there to resolve our tensions and does what she was designed to do is proved by the tranquillity in which she leaves us as we close the book.

This major drama of tensions and resolutions is accompanied by many minor dramas of the same kind. In the hospital scene, for example, there is a reference to the voluptuous loveliness that "Lafayette has limned for ages yet to come." Who is this Lafayette and what loveliness? This mystery keeps us in suspense, but we are relieved at last; for there are no loose ends in *Ulysses*. We discover about two hundred pages later that Lafayette is a Dublin photographer who took a picture of Mrs. Bloom, the same, in fact, that Mr. Bloom carries around with him to show to strangers.

If *Ulysses* is radiant, it must be harmonious. Burke's pattern of psychological responses does not account for all Joyce meant by harmony. Meaning more than tension resolved, harmony seems to imply musical organization and development. Perhaps Joyce's works, in some way analogous to music, achieve some of music's effects. *Ulysses* resembles a symphony or a suite in the sense of being an intricate structure of rhythm, sound, recurrence, and variation, in which each part has its key and tonal quality, and part is linked to part by developing themes. *Ulysses* is not music, however, but literature, and all these musical devices are those of poetry. The harmony of part and whole that Joyce intended is common to the several arts. He took the term from music since harmony is plainest there or, it may be, since all the arts, as Pater observed, aspire to the condition of music.

Thematic connections help give *Ulysses* its massive unity and its harmonious coherence. When Frank Budgen pointed out that "crosstrees" is not the proper word for the yard of a schooner, Joyce thanked him and replied that he could not change it because it comes in later on. The reappearance of crosstrees is perhaps the simplest of these interconnections. The potato and the cake of soap that Mr. Bloom carries about with him all day are more elaborate. Emerging at last in the brothel and in the kitchen, the one preserves his manhood and the other washes his guilt away. At once significant and structural, such themes compose the grand design. Sometimes they lie alongside one another and sometimes, developing, they intertwine. The brasses of Mrs. Bloom's bed jingle when Boylan's letter comes. The jaunting car jingles as it carries Boylan to that bed. There, one jingle, uniting with the other, develops into "jigajiga."

The brothel episode, where this development occurs, serves as a great thematic junction. As Bloom and Stephen search the deposits of memory, all themes that have bound the day together reappear, composing a nightmare for those heroes and for the book a structural center. But a more comprehensive view of the whole, its parts, and their inter-relationship is afforded by the cross-section of Dublin in the episode of the Wandering Rocks. Here, eighteen brief episodes, each distinguished by tone and rhythm, and each connected with the others by reference and theme, form an epitome of the book. Serving to recapitulate the eighteen episodes, a nineteenth assures their harmony.

This musical sequence with its coda introduces a more elaborate musical structure, the scene in the Ormond Hotel or the chapter of Sirens. To support the parallel of Homer's singing ladies by means of a fugue is not inappropriate. The catalogue of fragments at the beginning of this chapter is a kind of prelude and at the same time an index of the themes that, fleeing from and pursuing one another, compose the fugue. Arranging the materials of this chapter according to musical laws, Joyce created, if not a fugue, a fugal structure in which he anticipated many of the contrapuntal effects of *Finnegans Wake*. Treatment, theme, and sound conspire as Dollard barreltones "The Croppy Boy": "Chordsdark. Lugugugubrious . . . Croak of vast manless moonless womoonless marsh." To these profound harmonies Mr. Bloom's instrument pipes a slight conclusion. Musical development shapes the parts of this orchestral harmony and even determines the order of the words: Miss Kennedy, at once barmaid and Siren, "sauntered sadly from bright light, twining a loose hair behind an ear. Sauntering sadly, gold no more, she twisted twined a hair.

Sadly she twined in sauntering gold hair behind a curving ear."
As music symbolizes the form of our feeling, this verbal pattern
symbolizes the form of music.

Since the chapter itself forms a fugue, it must express flight
and pursuit. Mr. Bloom avoids the barmaids as Odysseus avoided
the Sirens. Tempted to return to Mrs. Bloom, he resists; but
Boylan, although fleeing the Sirens, pursues Mrs. Bloom. The
barmaids, Bloom, and Boylan are perhaps the three voices of this
fugue, but other voices echo theirs, and the sounds, moods, and
tones of Joyce's poetry, supporting and expressing the characters,
compose another fugal pattern. As the form of the hospital scene,
symbolizing more than embryonic development, suggests all circular development, so this fugal arrangement of sounds and
characters suggests the condition and development of art.

When music tries to be literature, the results are sometimes
neither music nor literature. Program music is one result and
Wagnerian opera another. When literature tries to be music, the
results are sometimes almost as doubtful. In his poem of Peter
Quince, Wallace Stevens tried to make statement do the work
of sound. Composing a pseudo-quartet, he anticipated the *Four
Quartets* of Eliot. That both are good poems has little to do,
however, with any art but poetry. Aldous Huxley in *Point Counter
Point* and many others from the time of Mallarmé to our own
have shown a nostalgia for the condition of music. The arts may
continue to aspire, but since each of them is a symbolic form,
each does what no other can do. The difference between music
and literature is that literature, composed of words, has subject
matter. In music sound is form, but in literature meaning is form.
Aping music, literature may acquire an alien structure or, at best,
improve in sound and rhythm, the elements it shares with music.
In his formal experiment of the Sirens, Joyce did not achieve
music, but he symbolized music and made a pattern of sound and
rhythm like nothing else in the world.

As Joyce could do anything with words, so he could do anything with rhythm and tone, the other elements of his art. Like his
creator, young Stephen of *A Portrait of the Artist* preferred the
"poise and balance of the period" to its color. In the largest sense,

rhythm is the structural harmony of part and part, but rhythm, indistinguishable from tone, is also the substance of the part. Providing the structure of the Laestrygonian episode, rhythm and tone are its meaning. The rhythm and tone with which Joyce expressed Father Conmee's walk through the city in the Wandering Rocks are Father Conmee. His grave, ordered, passionless life is not stated but symbolized by the quality of the prose. Rhythm and tone are the character of Gerty MacDowell. To express the meaning of *Dubliners* Joyce chose what he called "a style of scrupulous meanness." In *A Portrait of the Artist* he presented Stephen's aesthetic experience in a warm, juicy style that carries both Stephen's adolescent rapture and Joyce's irony. Anna Livia Plurabelle and sometimes Shem, her favorite son, consist of anapaests. Each theme of *Finnegans Wake* has its proper rhythm and its tone. In elaborate harmony, these themes compose what I. A. Richards, speaking of Eliot, called the "music of ideas." This music, like Milton's, reaches the mind by way of the ear.

Ulysses and *Finnegans Wake,* for all their obsessive concern with pride and guilt, are genial books. Pain and all the trouble of the night, transmuted by understanding and acceptance, have become materials for art, distant now from self. Here again we must separate life from art. Reappearing in art, the horrors of life, have become elements in a joyous, impersonal structure. The dominant tone of Joyce's great harmonies of sound and rhythm is one of brightness and gaiety.

In his Paris notebook, Joyce called comedy the greatest of arts because the joy of comedy is freest from desire or loathing. He admired the elegance and humor of Chaucer as he admired the humor of Sterne and the wit of Swift. Their powers and the comic spirit were also his. Joyce was astonished that critics of his work failed to find it funny.

The wit of Swift prevented his worldly success. Sterne's Parson Yorick, who was honest, gay, and witty, was denied the preferment he deserved because, thinking gravity "a mysterious carriage of the body to cover the defects of the mind," he told the truth with levity. If the eighteenth century, supposedly the age of wit, found Swift and Sterne too witty, the plight of Joyce in our age was more desperate. Never needing the assurance of a crowd, he stood apart from those who are not only solemn but serious about it. Yet, like Shaw, Joyce was most serious and most profound when at his gayest. His humor is the proof of understanding and the sign of equanimity.

LIFE AND WORKS

1882 Joyce born in Dublin (February 2)
1888 Enters Clongowes Wood College
1893 Enters Belvedere College
1898 Enters University College
1900 "Ibsen's New Drama," *Fortnightly Review,* CCCC, 575–90 (April 1)
1901 *The Day of the Rabblement* (pamphlet), Dublin
1902 Essay on Mangan, *St. Stephen's* magazine (May). Leaves Dublin for Paris upon graduation
1903 Returns to Dublin. Mother dies
1904 Leaves Dublin with Nora Barnacle. Teaches English in Berlitz School, Trieste. *The Holy Office* (broadside)
1907 *Chamber Music,* London, Elkin Mathews
1912 *Gas from a Burner* (broadside)
1914 *Dubliners,* London, Grant Richards
1915 Settles in Zürich
1916 *A Portrait of the Artist as a Young Man,* New York, B. W. Huebsch
1918 *Exiles,* London, Grant Richards
1920 Settles in Paris
1922 *Ulysses,* Paris, Shakespeare and Company
1927 *Pomes Penyeach,* Paris, Shakespeare and Company
1933 Federal Judge John M. Woolsey permits publication of *Ulysses* in United States
1939 *Finnegans Wake,* London, Faber & Faber; New York, Viking Press
1941 Dies in Zürich (January 13)
1944 *Stephen Hero,* New York, New Directions

BIBLIOGRAPHY

Beckett, Samuel, and others, *Our Exagmination* . . . , Paris, Shakespeare and Company, 1929; reprinted as *An Exagmination* . . . , Norfolk, Conn., New Directions, 1939 (Essays on *Finnegans Wake*).

Budgen, Frank, *James Joyce and the Making of "Ulysses,"* New York, Harrison Smith, 1934 (The best book on *Ulysses*).

Campbell, Joseph, and Robinson, Henry Morton, *A Skeleton Key to "Finnegans Wake,"* New York, Harcourt, Brace, 1944.

Gilbert, Stuart, *James Joyce's "Ulysses,"* London, Faber & Faber, 1930.

Givens, Seon, editor, *James Joyce: Two Decades of Criticism,* New York, Vanguard, 1948 (Essays by Budgen, Campbell, Damon, Eliot, Farrell, Gilbert, Jolas, Wilson, and others).

Gorman, Herbert, *James Joyce,* New York, Farrar & Rinehart, 1939; reprinted 1949 (Biography. Contains letters, essays, journals, verses by Joyce).

Levin, Harry, *James Joyce,* Norfolk, Conn., New Directions, 1941 (A critical survey).

SELECTIVE INDEX

THIS BOOK MAY BE KEPT

14 Days

and may be renewed if not called for by
someone else.
A fine of 2¢ per day is charged if the book
is kept after the last date stamped below.

DUE	DUE	DUE
APR 1 8 1992		